Starting Over . . . Again

By Rick Cottrell

All Scripture quotations are taken
from the Holy Bible, *King James Version.*

DEDICATION

- To my Aunt Dais who was there in the beginning. She asked the probing questions, and then helped me find the answers during our many personal Bible studies together. She always lent an ear and shared an encouraging word that helped shape my future.

- To my wonderful wife, Pam, who knows all my many faults and loves me anyway. A God-given gift that keeps me on the straight and narrow. She is the love of my life.

- To my two lovely girls, Brittany and Kelly, arrows in my quiver, sharp, straight, and true, of whom I could not be more proud.

CONTENTS

FOREWORD

Rick Cottrell is a fully devoted follower of Christ, a pastor committed to making disciples, and a visionary who knows that we can be, "more than conquerors through Him that loved us [and gave Himself for us]" (Romans 8:37). Rick is husband to Pam and the father of Brittany and Kelly. Each member of the Cottrell family is a living example of God's grace and keeping power. Pam, Brittany, and Kelly are dynamic Christians touching lives in the church and community. It was an honor to work with Rick and his family as we ministered to thousands of young people in summer camps for four years. Their sacrifice to minister to others was inspiring to all who observed.

Pastor Cottrell has observed people who once prayed in the altars, sang in the choir, taught Sunday school, and testified of God's saving grace to those who had fallen back into the grip of sin. As a pastor, he has seen many lives transformed, grow in Christ, and become fully devoted followers of Jesus. However, too often he has seen the failures of many who have gone back to the world of sin and bondage. It is out of his passion for helping people become victorious followers of Jesus that Pastor Cottrell writes, *Starting Over . . . Again*. His message is clear. God loves the backslider and calls him or her to start over, again. Rick draws on his personal experience of walking with Christ for 38 years while encouraging, challenging, and with clarity, mapping out a path to victorious living and dying in Christ.

If you want to get started right, have a plan for victorious living, and fulfill your divine destiny; I recommend *Starting Over . . . Again.*

–David H. Gosnell

PREFACE

Having been SAVED for over 38 years, I can truly testify that there is nothing like the Christian journey. There is freshness to each morning and sense of fulfillment at the end of every day when you are in the will of God. My mind is made up to follow the Lord. My heart and soul belong to Jesus Christ. I have relinquished control of my life into His hands. I belong to Him. If I woke up in the morning and there was an announcement from God that there was no heaven or hell, I would not change a thing. This would still be the life for me. Truly, the journey gets sweeter and sweeter as the days go by.

I have not always enjoyed this confidence in Christ. My first steps as a Christian believer were very unstable. Having given my heart to Christ on August 9, 1975, at a little Baptist church in Illinois, I knew I was on a journey but had no sense of direction. I knew I had a new life but didn't know what to do with it. I was up one minute and down the next with more failures than successes. The average Christian wouldn't have given me much hope. I failed forward from one frustration to another and found myself starting over again and again.

It was at that point my Aunt Dais came along beside me as a partner and we spent countless nights in Bible study, listening to preaching tapes, and we had open discussion concerning our new walk in Christ. As I look back, I can clearly see how important these times were in grounding me in the Christian faith. Even before I knew what a covenant partner was, she was one to me.

Certain foundational standards begin to kick in and I was getting stronger and stronger in the spirit. As you read through the pages of my heart, I want to share with you some of those core principles that I know will root and ground you firmly in the faith as they have helped me.

Several years serving as a pastor, I have observed those who have struggled in their Christian walk and some have failed to the point of going back on God. Hoping they will return, I take pen in hand to lend support and direction in their next effort to wholly follow the Lord.

War has been declared against Christians on every front. Many have been wounded, some have deserted, and others are being held captive by the enemy. However, I believe in the God of a second chance, the Lord of everlasting mercy, the Jesus who is full of grace, and the hope of glory. Christ our Savior stands calling for the backslider to return unto Him. He is the good Father who waits for the Prodigal to come home. His caring arms are open wide and there is a place reserved by His side for all who will make the trip.

Throughout this book, strategic foundational principles will be shared that will position the disciple in the truth of God. The principles that are considered in these pages are basic Christian disciplines and need to be established early in the Christian walk.

It is my hope and prayer that this book will serve as a spiritual primer for your Christian walk and a reference guide in time to come. It is written for the backslider who has come home but it is also a discipleship tool for all to refresh themselves in the core values of the Christian walk. Read it slowly and digest it thoroughly.

INTRODUCTION
Starting Over . . . Again

The altar call has been given, some have responded. Among the souls who have come forward this morning is Alice. She is on her knees before God. Her words are coming slowly. She is *emotionally torn. It is evident that Alice is frustrated.*

As her pastor I ask, "Alice, can I help you pray for something this morning?" She responds, "Pastor, I need to rededicate my life back to God. I have been living in sin. I know that I shouldn't have drifted away and I am not sure if I can make it this time. I feel like such a failure. Please pray for me to make it."

This scenario has been repeated over and over during the course of my ministry. The names and the stories were different but the issues were the same.

If you are reading this, there's a good chance that you, like Alice, have at times seen the need to rededicate your life back to Christ. Most likely, you were "born again" at an earlier time and for one reason or another you found yourself backslidden on the Lord. When I say *backslidden*, I mean you went backwards instead of forwards in your journey as a believer. We could spend the next several chapters discussing the validity of the question, "Can a saved person backslide?" You may have already answered that question in your own personal journey. For the sake of scriptural soundness to the question consider the following.

Now the just shall live by faith: but if any man draw back, my soul shall have no pleasure in him. But we are not of them who draw back unto perdition; but of them that believe to the saving of the soul (Hebrews 10:38-39).

Having damnation, because they have cast off their first faith (1 Timothy 5:12).

For if God spared not the natural branches, take heed lest he also spare not thee. Behold therefore the goodness and severity of God: on them which fell, severity; but toward thee, goodness, if thou continue in his goodness: otherwise thou also shalt be cut off (Romans 11:21-22).

The word *backslider* is used one time in the Bible. The word *backsliding* is used 12 times in the Scriptures. Besides this:

> You can *shipwreck* your faith (1 Timothy 1:19).
> You can *cast off* your faith (1 Timothy 5:12).
> You can become *entangled* in sin again (2 Peter 2:20).
> You can be *overcome* (2 Peter 2:20).
> You can become like a dog *going back* to his vomit (2 Peter 2:22).
> You can become like a pig *going back* to the mire (2 Peter 2:22).
> You can be a *castaway* (1 Corinthians 9:27).

Backsliding happens! We can be thankful that God has a plan for the backslider. He remakes the cracked pot. He puts us back on the wheel. When our faith is derailed, He gets us back on track. We are the sheep who have a tendency to go astray. He is the Good Shepherd who listens for our call of help. He is ready to heal our hurt and return us to the fold. He will readily leave the 99 and look for the one that has drifted away. The backslider needs to be found quickly.

A voice was heard upon the high places, weeping and supplications of the children of Israel: for they have perverted their way, and they have forgotten the Lord their God. Return, ye backsliding children, and I will heal your backslidings. Behold, we come unto thee; for thou art the Lord our God (Jeremiah 3:21-22).

The harsh reality is that when you backslide, you let God, yourself, and your peers down. When it happens we can understand the devastation it brings to our witness and our life. How did this happen to me? What could I have done differently? What can I do so I will never go back on God again? There are many reasons we stumble and fall in the Christian walk. Let us consider the following:

You may have failed to . . .
- Count the cost of your salvation.
- Recognize the deception of your enemy.
- Obtain a mentor and covenant partner.
- Include the benefit of attending a good church.
- Have a daily time of prayer.
- Read your Bible.
- Separate yourself from your old life.

11

- ❏ Discern the difference between temptation and tribulation.
- ❏ Understand that you were saved to give not just receive.
- ❏ Realize that some of God's greatest failed at times.

Whether one of these was a difficulty or not, we can be better prepared for our journey with God if we consider each one carefully. This book has found its way into your hands. Read it and process it slowly. Let its contents become the principles that you live by.

Let's look at each of these accounts and learn from the mistakes of others and ourselves. It has been said that a mistake is only a mistake if we fail to learn something in the process. So, after a mistake we should ask the question, "What did I learn?" This is what we will ask ourselves as we journey on.

It has also been said, "A mistake is only a mistake if you make it twice." Thank God for His grace and mercy and that He is the God of a second chance and a third and a fourth. When you think about it, even God started over . . . at least once. He wiped the slate clean and started again with Noah and his family. God designed this world with "starting over" in mind. Every 24 hours there is a new day, every month begins with one, every seven days we start a new week and it begins with Sunday, and every 365 days we have a new year. In the near future, God will start over again with a new heaven and a new earth. It's okay for you to start over, again. He has given you another opportunity to move forward in the Kingdom so let's make the best of it.

We will use several scriptures throughout this book. The Word of God is extremely important in our Christian walk. It is so important that you must read the scriptures at a snail's pace and let them take root into your spirit.

CHAPTER ONE

COUNT THE COST OF YOUR SALVATION

If any man come to me, and hate not his father, and mother, and wife, and children, and brethren, and sisters, yea, and his own life also, he cannot be my disciple. And whosoever doth not bear his cross, and come after me, cannot be my disciple. For which of you, intending to build a tower, sitteth not down first, and **counteth the cost**, *whether he have sufficient to finish it? Lest haply,* **after he hath laid the foundation**, *and is not able to finish it, all that behold it begin to mock him, Saying, This man began to build, and was not able to finish* (Luke 14:26-30).

Probably the hardest part of the journey is the beginning and the biggest battle is fought in the mind. It doesn't help if we are deluded and confused about what we are doing. When I was born again, I didn't really sell out to God, the fact is, I was purchased by God. There was a high price that was paid for my salvation. My life was a life of bondage in sin and the Lord purchased me from that life of slavery.

For ye are bought with a price: therefore glorify God in your body, and in your spirit, which are God's (1 Corinthians 6:20).

The price for the redemption of my soul was very high. I was not worth what God had to pay. The Lord Jesus was sold for 30 pieces of silver. That was the bargain of the century. You and I were purchased with the price of a life; the Son of God's life. For this gift to humanity, the world valued at 30 pieces of silver, yet one drop of His blood would save the life of untold millions.

*Then Judas, which had betrayeth him, when he saw that he was condemned, repented himself, and brought again the **thirty pieces of silver** to the chief priests and elders, Saying, "I have sinned in that I have betrayed the innocent blood." And they said, "what is that to us? see thou to that." And he cast down the pieces of silver in the temple, and departed, and went and hanged himself. And the chief priests took the silver pieces, and said, "It is not lawful for to put them into the treasury, because it is the **price of blood"** (Matthew 27:3-6).*

It was not just any life; it was the life of God's Son. It was not just a son; or one of many, but it was God's *only* Son.

God in heaven must have cared a lot about you. Your value is solidified by His willingness to pay such a high price on your behalf. Surely we can see God's love demonstrated to us by the giving of His only Son and Christ dying for us while we were still sinners. Before we got cleaned up, He loved us. While I resisted and cursed, He pursued me with passion and persistence. Thank God that while we were still in sin, He loved us.

Yet also, His love is also confirmed in the fact that He chastises and corrects us (Hebrews 12:6). We are truly His sons and daughters. He loves us enough *not* to let go. The nagging conviction we feel when we abandon Him is evident that He is pursuing us. As the psalmist David said, "Surly goodness and mercy shall follow me all the days of my life and I will dwell in the house of the Lord forever" (Psalms 23:6). Every time I have stumbled and fallen, His goodness and His mercy were there to pick me up again. When you and I make it to our home in heaven, we will walk through those pearly gates with goodness on one arm and mercy on the other. That is how much God loves us.

For God so loved the world, that he gave his only begotten Son, that whosoever believeth in him should not perish, but have everlasting life (John 3:16).

Salvation to us is 100 percent free. It was paid in full through the death of Christ. However, if you are going to be

17

successful in your walk with the Lord, you must also understand there will be a cost to us. Again, the price of our salvation was completely paid by the Lord and we cannot do anything to buy it. Even if it were possible to purchase salvation, there are none who could afford the price. However, as we continue on in our walk with God there will be a price to be paid. Consider the following scriptures.

THE COST OF LIVING GODLY

Yea, and all that will live godly in Christ Jesus shall suffer persecution (2 Timothy 3:12).

We suffer for many reasons. Many times we suffer because of our own faults and mistakes. However even if we did everything right, we must understand that we will at times suffer persecution for just being a Christian. You will be persecuted by the enemy because every time he sees you, he is reminded of Christ. You will be persecuted by the world because you are a reminder of their disobedience to God. We are not of this world. We are aliens, strangers, and foreigners. So many times people strike out against what they don't understand and fight against that which is different.

THE COST OF FOLLOWING CHRIST

Then said Jesus unto his disciples, "If any man will come after me, let him deny himself, and take up his cross, and follow me" (Matthew 16:24).

The civil leaders had no respect for Christ. The religious leaders hated Christ. They worked together to crucify Him. Today there is an increasing hatred and disrespect among the world and government concerning Christians. This world is anti-Christ in nature. We must carry our cross and be ready for the same treatment that Christ received at the hands of the world. Often I am asked, "How's the world treating you?" and I usually respond, "Better than I expect." I expect nothing from this world. What good I receive is because of my God. John the apostle warned us, "In the world ye shall have tribulation." Jesus himself warned us in John 15:18-19, "If the world hate you, ye know that it hated me before it hated you. If ye were of the world, the world would love his own: but because ye are not of the world, but I have chosen you out of the world, therefore the world hateth you." The world hated Christ and it will hate you when you follow Him.

THE COST IS MY LIFE.

For whosoever will save his life shall lose it: and whosoever will lose his life for my sake shall find it. For what is a man profited, if he shall gain the whole world, and lose his own soul? or what shall a man give in exchange for his soul? (Matthew 16:25-26).

We must be crucified with Christ. If we are dead already, then our expectations and feelings are null and void. To give this short life to Christ would be my reasonable service. I do realize that there is a wider path to take. There is a broad way that many are travelling. It is easy to fall in step with the crowd and lose your direction, but at the end of the road is hell. There is a narrow path that we must look for. We must pay attention in order to stay on this course, but it will be worth all the problems that we encounter when we get to the end of the journey. On this expedition most of us will never be called upon to die for our faith; however, we are challenged to live for God. This is the greatest test of our faith for here we die daily as we carry our cross and follow our Lord. Wherever He leads we must follow. We must follow in His steps.

As I follow Him, my life will change. Every day I will die a little more and He will live in me a little more. Every day I will learn to love those who hate me, pray for those who persecute me and bless those who curse me. The cost is my life which was worthless before Christ anyway.

THE COST IS NOTHING COMPARED TO THE GLORY.

> *For I reckon that the sufferings of this present time are not worthy to be compared with the glory which shall be revealed in us* (Romans 8:18).

Eternity will be a long time. Christ has gone to prepare a place for us to be with Him in eternity. This is a special place. The scripture says that our eyes have not seen and our ears have not heard the things that God has prepared for us. Ten seconds inside heaven will be all the time we need to forget all the hurts of this world. The old song says, *It will be joy unspeakable and full of glory . . . and the half has never yet been told.*

Therefore I endure all things for the elect's sakes, that they may also obtain the salvation which is in Christ Jesus with eternal glory (2 Timothy 2:10).

Oh yes, there is a cost. For sure there is a price to be paid. It may seem high at times but in the end, it will be the deal of our lifetime. Just a short life of investing into the kingdom of God will produce an eternity of dividends. You are laying up for yourself treasures in heaven. You may live as a pauper now but you will reign as a king and priest later. For there will be no tears, no sorrow, no pain, no sickness, no heartaches, no death, in heaven. What a bargain!

While we are counting the cost we need to consider the cost of *not* serving the Lord. The enemy also pays a dividend if you will serve him. The Bible says, "For the wages of sin is death" All of the devil's escapades will lead us to death; sometimes a horrible and even quicker death because of the dangerous avenues where we find ourselves walking. Sometimes we experience a painful and diseased death due to the atmosphere of the journey with Satan.

Our enemy works as a deceiver. He never tells us the truth. He makes sin sound and look good but the end is death. The world plays up to a life of sexual promiscuity. They say, "If it feels good, do it" or "Everybody is doing it." The fact is that everybody is not doing it and those who are will suffer the disaster of divorce, damage of diseases, ruptured relationships with their spouse, children, or both, and often times the perpetrator of the sin cannot live with the pain they caused others. If they survive the embarrassment, they tote the baggage around the rest of their lives.

21

How many has the devil told that *one* drink or *one* drug won't hurt anyone? It is only a couple of beers! It is only marijuana! Country music singer Country Dick Montana was known as an out of control beer-swigging, party-showman. One of the songs on his first and only album was, "It's Only Cocaine." Just two months after completing the album on November 8, 1995, he died in his boots, onstage at the Longhorn Cabaret in Whistler, British Columbia, of an aortic aneurysm while playing a song called "The Girl I Almost Married." The title of his album was "The Devil Lied to Me." He was 40 years old.

My mother accepted Christ as her Savior at an early age, married my dad at 15 years old. I came along pretty soon and we had a family. She took a wrong turn somewhere and chose to test the waters of sin. After leaving home she quickly became a severe alcoholic and a drug user. She abused herself and was abused by others. The waters of sin quickly drowned her and took her life at the young age of 48 years old. It all started with one drink and one party. The cost of living ungodly was a lost future that included me and her grandchildren. She didn't get to be a part of their lives. What a high price to pay.

We must remember that the enemy comes to kill, steal, and destroy but God comes to give abundant life. We need to count the cost. The Christian should not operate in deception. Too many Christians have joined up with the team but have not been told that there is an opponent. The life of the Christian is not all trouble but there will be some along the way. The roses are not without thorns. If we understand this, we will be prepared for the battle and will not be taken by surprise. We are winners. We are conquerors. Matter of fact, Romans 8:37 say, "Nay, in all these things we are more than conquerors through him that loved us."

The great revivalist Leonard Ravenhill, was preaching on this very text. He said,

> *This man says we are more than conquerors. You know, when those three Hebrew children went into a burning, fiery furnace, they were conquerors. But when . . . they walked out, they were more than conquerors.*

> *When Daniel went into the lion's den, he was a conqueror. But when they pulled him out and made them change the laws of the Medes and the Persians, he was more than a conqueror.*

> *When Jesus went to the cross . . . When He went to the grave with the sin of the world He was a conqueror. When He rose from the dead he was more than a conqueror.*

The point! When one is destroyed by persecution he is a conqueror, but when he is victorious through the persecution, he is *more than a conqueror*. **You will be also.** Keep marching on. You are designed to be more than a conqueror!

A GOOD HABIT TO GET YOU BACK ON TRACK

BE THANKFUL EVERY DAY

Christ paid a supreme price for me.
The least I could do is be thankful.
thanks be unto God for his unspeakable gift
(2 Corinthians 9:15).

Some Ways to Practice Thankfulness

1. Keep a Gratitude Journal.
2. Send a thank-you note to someone who has positively affected your life.
3. Make a top-ten list of things for which you are thankful.
4. Instead of focusing on what you don't have, enumerate what you do have.
5. Pray a thankful prayer.
6. Do something good in tribute of a deceased friend or family member to honor them.

REFLECTION POINTS

1. God paid an extreme price for our salvation. He gave His only son on a cruel cross. Write a short prayer to God thanking Him for what He did for you.

_____

_____

_____

_____

_____

2. I know you are thankful for what the Lord has done for you. List the top 10 things you are thankful for.

1. _____
2. _____
3. _____
4. _____
5. _____
6. _____
7. _____
8. _____
9. _____
10. _____

CHAPTER TWO

RECOGNIZE THE DECEPTION
OF YOUR ENEMY

We must realize that we will be tempted.

When we come to God and are born again, we are surrounded by rejoicing and excitement. It is natural to think that all is good and the future is bright. This is true; however, at the very moment that we accept the Savior, we also denounce our old master the devil. He is not happy with losing one of his. Satan, who is a deceiver at heart, will set in motion a plan to get you back. He is very patient but he has a recognizable process that he uses. A person will backslide in steps. With each step, we move away from God, our eyes become a little dimmer, our ears are a little duller and our heart a little harder. We need to recognize the devices and the deception of the devil quickly.

Temptation in itself is not sin. When we give in then it becomes sin. The good news is that if you sin, there is a remedy for your sin.

> *If we confess our sins, he is faithful and just to forgive us our sins, and to cleanse us from all unrighteousness* (1 John 1:9).

> *My little children, these things write I unto you, that ye sin not. And if any man sin, we have an advocate with the Father, Jesus Christ the righteous* (1 John 2:1).

An advocate means an intercessor. As our advocate, Christ intercedes to God the Father on our behalf. Christ is the son of God but He also was human; therefore, He understands our situations and troubles. He feels your pain and heartache. Do your best not to sin, but if you do, remember that there is a solution to the pollution of sin, the cleansing blood of Jesus Christ.

> *People will sin, this is sure,*
> *The devil is the cause but Christ is the cure!*

When we fail, we must listen to what God has said, "we have an advocate" and run to God instead of running from God. Do not listen to the devil. He is a deceiver and a liar.

When you fail, the devil will try to tell you:

What you did wasn't wrong.
OR

Maybe it was wrong, but it's no big deal.
AND
God doesn't love you anymore.
AND
It's no use trying again.

Most falls begin with a stumble. A person will backslide in stages and the earlier you recognize the deception of the devil, the easier it will be to rebuke him for the liar that he is.

The enemy has a plan to deceive us all but we are not ignorant concerning his devices. He has a modus operandi or M.O. that he uses time and again. He used it in the Garden of Eden and he will use it on you. Let's look at the first temptation and how quickly the old serpent leads them through the process of deception that leads to the fall of man found in Genesis, chapter 3.

Now the serpent was more subtil than any beast of the field which the Lord God had made. And he said unto the woman, "Yea, hath God said, 'Ye shall not eat of every tree of the garden'"?

And the woman said unto the serpent, "We may eat of the fruit of the trees of the garden: But of the fruit of the tree which is in the midst of the garden, God hath said, 'Ye shall not eat of it, neither shall ye touch it, lest ye die.'" And the serpent said unto the woman, "Ye shall not surely die: For God doth know that in the day ye eat thereof, then your eyes shall be opened, and ye shall be as gods, knowing good and evil." And when the woman saw that the tree was good for food, and that it was pleasant to the eyes, and a tree to be desired to make one wise, she took of the fruit thereof, and did eat, and gave also unto her husband with her; and he did eat. And the eyes of them both were opened, and they knew that they were naked; and they sewed fig leaves together, and made themselves aprons. And they heard the voice of the Lord God walking in the garden in the cool of the day: and Adam and his wife hid themselves from the presence of the Lord God amongst the trees of the garden. And the Lord God called unto Adam, and said unto him, "Where art thou?" (vv. 1-9)

The first step is what I call the **Conception of Deception.** This is the initial seed that he will plant and try to get it to grow. In Genesis 3:1, ". . . and he said unto the woman . . .," He wants to talk and he wants you to listen. He won't come in a red suit with a pitchfork breathing fire. No, he will usually speak to you through an old acquaintance or someone you trust. Here in Genesis he spoke to Eve through a "subtil" serpent. "Subtil" means cunning and crafty.

Like Eve, the devil starts talking to us and it is hard to recognize who he is. When you first got saved everybody and everything looked and felt great. The church seemed so perfect and all the people were saints. Now you are not sure. The devil starts to talk. I wonder about that preacher? Who are the hypocrites? Are they out to get my money? She thinks you're a hypocrite! Don't you miss the old friends and the parties?

He may even cause someone to hurt your feelings or make you upset. Then the seed of deception is planted. We need to remove it now before it takes root and raises itself up. Ephesians 4:26-27 says, "Be ye angry, and sin not: let not the sun go down upon your wrath: Neither give place to the devil." If we give him a place, he will set up a command center. Give him an inch he will become a ruler. His only power is deception. The problem with deception is that it is very deceiving. We must take control of the situation quickly. If we don't take control, he will.

The second step is our **Selection of Reception.** In this phase, the enemy will tune us in to hear and trust only him. He asked Eve, "Did God really say that?" *He must* get you to tune out God's Word. God will try to speak to us in many ways but we have to listen. He will speak through the preacher, the Bible, a covenant partner, mentor, or even a song. You can have ears but not be able to hear. When God was speaking to the seven churches in Revelation, He said over and over, "he that hath an ear, let him hear." Hear what the Word says. We must resist the devil. Fight the good fight of faith. Lay hold on eternal life.

LISTEN TO JAMES
Submit yourselves therefore to God. Resist the devil, and he will flee from you (James 4:7).

LISTEN TO PETER
Be sober, be vigilant; because your adversary the devil, as a roaring lion, walketh about, seeking whom he may devour (1 Peter 5:8).

LISTEN TO PAUL

Neither give place to the devil (Ephesians 4:27).

LISTEN TO JOHN

And the great dragon was cast out, that old serpent, called the Devil, and Satan, which deceiveth the whole world: he was cast out into the earth, and his angels were cast out with him (Revelation 12:9).

> THE DEVIL IS A DECEIVER.
>
> The trouble with deception is that it is very deceiving.

When our ears have stopped hearing and the reception has been hindered one would think that the devil would be happy with his success. The enemy is never satisfied. He continues with his domination of your life.

The third stage is the **Deflection of Our Perception.** The devil said to Eve, "Ye shalt not surely die." Now the devil directly attacked the Word of God. He has escalated His pace. Everything becomes another person's fault. We accept no blame for our actions. "If God hadn't put the tree in the garden in the first place, I could not have sinned. They didn't even shake my hand at church today." It doesn't matter that you shook nobody's hand! It is still their fault. Our perception of reality has been distorted. We have allowed the enemy to isolate us. When a person enters a cave of isolation, everything looks different. The sun is still shining but we can't see it because we are in a cave.

The general perceptions of people are many times centered on themselves. This is why it is so much easier to see someone else's faults than our own. My sin doesn't look as bad on me as it does on somebody else. Isn't it funny that

32

everyone driving slower than us on the freeway is an idiot and everyone driving faster is in too big a hurry. We tend to measure proper speed by ourselves rather than the speed limit set by law. So it is when we move away from God's law and set the limits by my situations and feelings. We must look at our situation through the eyes of Scripture. We are what it says we are. We can have what it says and do what it says we can do. If the Scripture says that the sun is shining then it doesn't matter how deep in the cave I am or how damp I feel, you'd better get out the sunblock if you go outside.

The fourth stage is the continual **Regression of Affection**. Adam and Eve, "They hid themselves from the presence of the Lord." It will get worse until we either quit church or rebel against the church. Either way we are backslid on God. Our affection toward God and others has changed. We will find ourselves saying, "My pastor just doesn't preach like he used to. The church isn't as friendly as it once was. They're only in it for the money. All he ever preaches about is tithes and me. They are nothing but a bunch of hypocrites." Finally, we end up hiding from God and he is asking, "Where art thou?"

We find ourselves on the outside looking in. We don't know how it happened or exactly when it happened but we have backslid. What changed? Was it the church? No, the church has always had its troubles but it has the same troubles now as when you first started attending. Was it God? No. God is the same yesterday, today and forever. Then who has changed? You did.

You see, I don't find God because he is never lost. I am the one that gets lost. He comes looking for me because I am lost and hiding and says, "Where art thou?" He knows where I am. The question is not for Him—it is for me. He is calling to me because I am the agent of change for my life. It is up to me to accept responsibility for my life. So, face up and fess up, then get up and grow up and come out of hiding and serve the Lord.

GOOD HABIT

DON'T SPEND ANYTIME LISTENING TO THE DEVIL.

Now the serpent was more subtil than any beast of the field which the Lord God had made. And he said unto the woman . . . (Genesis 3:1).

It began with the devil talking and Eve listening. Even Christ wouldn't have extended conservation with the devil or those who he was speaking through.

But he turned, and said unto Peter, Get thee behind me, Satan: thou art an offence unto me: for thou savourest not the things that be of God, but those that be of men (Matthew 16:23).

When you recognize it is the devil talking, tell him immediately to get behind you. It will work.

REFLECTION POINTS

1. What are the four steps to backsliding?

   1) _____

   2) _____

   3) _____

   4) _____

2. Backsliding is a process. The enemy will try to deceive you. He told Eve that she would not die. When she sinned, the process of death began. The devil lied to her. What lie has he told you lately? He told me:

   _____

   _____

   _____

   _____

   _____

   _____

3. He has tried to get me to question or doubt the following? (Circle all that apply.)

   a) My pastor
   b) A member of the church
   c) My Christian walk
   d) The Bible
   e) A friend

35

CHAPTER THREE

OBTAIN A MENTOR AND
A COVENANT PARTNER

How think ye? If a man have an hundred sheep, and one of them be gone astray, doth he not leave the ninety and nine, and goeth into the mountains, and seeketh that which is gone astray? And if so be that he find it, verily I say unto you, he rejoiceth more of that sheep, than of the ninety and nine which went not astray (Matthew 18:12-13).

We are where we are because of who we follow. When we look behind us, we will see someone else following us. Everyone needs good mentors to follow.

They will help us to succeed and the next generation is depending on us to learn all we can. I owe much to those who have spoken into my life over the years. Some of my mentors have gone on to be with the Lord. Now, I find myself helping others with much of the same advice that assisted me.

Finding a **mentor** is choosing someone to be your spiritual guide. They will help you navigate through important decisions and many times will hold the key that unlocks the door to a better future. Ultimately this person is Christ. However, when you see persons who are following Christ and you admire their dedication, it is only natural to want to imitate them.

In 1 Thessalonians 1:6-7 the apostle Paul says,

> *And you became imitators of us and of the Lord, for in spite of persecution you received the word with joy inspired by the Holy Spirit, so that you became an example to all the believers in Macedonia and Achaia.*

The apostle Paul goes on to say in 2 Thessalonians. 3:7, "For yourselves know how ye ought to follow us: for we behaved not ourselves disorderly among you." And again in verse 9 he says, "Not because we have not power, but to make ourselves an ensample unto you to follow us." God has placed those in the body of Christ to lead and help us on our journey. We need not walk alone. We need the accountability.

The term *mentor* actually comes from Greek mythology. Odysseus, while away fighting in the Trojan War, left his son Telemachus under the tutelage of a wise man named Mentor.

38

Mentor's task was to provide an education of the soul and spirit, as well as the mind. Therefore, when Odysseus, the father, returned his son would be prepared for life. As we are awaiting the return of our Father, a mentor is an invaluable asset to being prepared for His return.

A **covenant partner** is someone you can share with and talk to. While the primary role of a mentor is to help you find the missing piece of the puzzle, a covenant partner will be the one to help you put the puzzle together. Covenant partners will take the time to look with you through the pieces and sort them out. They will rejoice with you at each piece that fits together. They will be friends who partner with you and help you on your journey. It needs to be someone you trust. I emphasize the word *help* because we don't need to surround ourselves with those who jeopardize and sabotage our faith. This relationship will take time to establish. You need to be on equal terms and there is no chief or boss. You help and support each other.

A mentor is like a coach while a covenant partner is a team player. A sports coach will encourage and instruct even though he is not playing the game himself. Your covenant partner plays the game with you. A mentor will help make a vessel seaworthy while your covenant partner will ride the ship of life with you and help you bail water if necessary.

> *Iron sharpeneth iron; so a man sharpeneth the countenance of his friend.*

There are all kinds of ships in this world and many times the ships that will take us through the storm are friendships.

Proverbs 27:17 says, "Iron sharpeneth iron; so a man sharpeneth the countenance of his friend." Your friends will either support your vision or strangle your dreams. The power of influence can never be underestimated. Your covenant partner may challenge some of your actions, but he will have your best interest in mind when he does.

David and Jonathan were covenant partners. Their relationship is recorded in the Scriptures. It is a tremendous story of friendship.

> *And it came to pass, when he had made an end of speaking unto Saul, that the soul of Jonathan was knit with the soul of David, and Jonathan loved him as his own soul* (1 Samuel 18:1).

> *Then Jonathan and David made a covenant, because he loved him as his own soul* (1 Samuel 18:3).

These two friends made a covenant together. They would take up for each other and even fight together. David's loyalty extended to Jonathan's children after he died. To be in covenant is a powerful thing.

A mentor is somewhat different and will bring different dynamics to the relationship. You must allow the mentor to speak into your life. We must allow them to hold us accountable. They not only teach us but also lead us. Sometimes we need someone who is separated from our problem and not emotionally attached to help guide us. They can see from a different perspective. Your mentor may be someone you follow from a distance. You may have more than

40

one mentor. I cannot stress enough the importance of having a mentor. You need at least one. Go get one. Choose him wisely but choose him soon.

Mentoring is a biblical principle.

- Christ mentored 12 disciples and told them they would do great works.
- Elijah mentored Elisha and he did twice the miracles of Elijah.
- Moses mentored Joshua and he entered the Promised Land but Moses did not.
- Paul mentored Timothy.

A mentor should make you a better person. A good mentor will pour himself into you without reservation. It will be apparent that the mentor operates in a supervisory role and it is understandable for you to feel like a subordinate while you are with him. It is to your benefit that you search and find a good mentor. A true mentor will not abuse his opportunity to speak into your life. You may find your mentor in your pastor or your Sunday school teacher. The mentor could be a relative such as a grandpa or grandma, aunt or uncle. You may have someone in mind right now. If not, begin to pray for God to bring a mentor and a covenant partner in your path.

GOOD HABIT

STAY IN CONTACT WITH YOUR COVENANT PARTNER OR MENTOR.

Maybe give him a call or have him call you on Sunday afternoon. This will provide the accountability that you need and give you a chance to discuss the Sunday service or sermon.

And let us consider one another to provoke unto love and to good works (Hebrews 10:24).

REFLECTION POINTS

1. Who do you consider to be your covenant partner?

_____

2. If you don't have a covenant partner, list a person you would consider.

_____

3. Who are your mentors?

    a) _____

    b) _____

    c) _____

4. If you have no mentor then think of someone you may consider and write that name down.

    a) _____

    b) _____

    c) _____

Now, make a plan to contact them. You need friends and assistance. Ask your pastor to help you find a covenant partner or mentor.

CHAPTER FOUR

INCLUDE THE BENEFIT OF ATTENDING A GOOD CHURCH

And let us consider one another to provoke unto love and to good works: Not forsaking the assembling of ourselves together, as the manner of some is; but exhorting one another: and so much the more, as ye see the day approaching (Hebrews 10:24-25).

I cannot say enough about the benefit of a good church. It is the vehicle that Christ left for us that will bring us to Him. It is not without its imperfections; however, it is the institution that Christ ordained for us to reach our full potential and our spiritual perfection. Ephesians 4:11-13 says,

*And he gave some, apostles; and some, prophets; and some, evangelists; and some, pastors and teachers; For the perfecting of the saints, for thy **work of the ministry, for the edifying of the body** of Christ: Till we all come in the unity of the faith, and of the knowledge of the Son of God, unto a perfect man, unto the measure of the stature of the fullness of Christ.*

The Church is the body of Christ and He is the head. We are the hands that touch the hurting for Him. We are the feet that go for Him. We are the ears that hear for Him. We have eyes that see for Him. In this world we are the instruments for His command. He is the head. He leads and directs and we obey. Nowhere is this better accomplished than through the Church.

And he is the head of the body, the church . . . that in all things he might have the preeminence (Colossians 1:18).

- Christ loves the Church.
- Christ gave Himself for the Church.
- Christ watches over the Church.
- Christ is coming back for the Church.

The body of Christ is your friends, your family, some will become a father or a mother. Others will be brothers and sisters. Occasionally like any family there will be disagreements and maybe even family feuds. In the end, we are family and family sticks together.

It is extremely important for you to surround yourself with people who will support and encourage you instead of tempting you to go back to your old life. Someone once said, "The company you keep will determine the trouble you meet." This is so true in your spiritual walk also. If you surround yourself by critics, you will become critical. If pessimists surround you, you will become cynical. On the other hand, if you attend a good church and surround yourself with faith, optimism, and hope you'll become a faithful idealist with a hopeful future.

There will always be the critics wherever you go. They will be on the job, up the street, and sometimes even at church. Don't let them speak into your life. Some will want to cut you down so they will look taller. Zig Ziglar said,

Don't be distracted by criticism. Remember, the only taste of success some people have is when they take a bite out of you.

Those who have a criticizing spirit will always be attacking others. They will criticize the pastor, deacon, leadership, and anyone else on the Kingdom team. The critic is on a team by himself. The critic will give you many reasons for not attending the house of God. They are often called excuses. Here is what I call the Big Four.

Excuse # 1
I CAN PRAY AT HOME.

We can and should pray at home. Most praying should be done at home. However, praying is not the only reason for attending church. There are many reasons for the Lord giving us the Church.

There is the **Fellowship Factor**. Isolation is a killer. The devil wants to isolate individuals so that he is the only voice that will be heard. We need the fellowship of other Christians. We are a community of believers. Remember, the fence that we build to shut others out will also shut us in. In the early church they were together regularly in prayer, the breaking of bread, and fellowship (Acts 2:42). We need each other.

In many circles we have reduced fellowship to eating and drinking. Fried chicken may have a part in a good time of fellowship, but if we leave a time of fellowship full in the belly but not enriched in the soul, we have done ourselves an injustice. There should be something dynamic and powerful when we come together in fellowship.

Two can do more than one. In Matthew 18:19-20 it says,

> *Again I say unto you, That if two of you shall agree on earth as touching any thing that they shall ask, it shall be done for them of my Father which is in heaven. For where two or three are gathered together in my name, there am I in the midst of them.*

Here we see that in the fellowship of two there is power in prayer and guaranteed participation with Christ. Rest assured that Christ participates in the fellowship of His saints. If anything is happening among the Body, He will be present. I hope you take every opportunity to be present also.

There is the **Dynamics of Discipleship**. As the body of Christ we need to grow. In order to grow, we need to eat. The church provides the table for our spiritual meals and our spiritual growth. Christ gave the church pastors and teachers for the perfecting of the saints and the work of the ministry. The church is our learning center. Learning requires discipline. Discipleship is involving oneself in teaching and modeling Christian disciplines. This involves everything from praying to God, to living right before Him. The church has many avenues to explore concerning discipleship. Sunday school, Bible study, small groups, and preaching are just a few of the tools of discipleship. One cannot just think of lunch and his hunger will be satisfied. No, the food has to be acquired, prepared, and eaten. This is the process. Our spiritual food is gathered and prepared by our teachers and ministers and we must come to the table and eat. This is the process. We call it church.

There is the **Act of Accountability.** We are our brother's keeper. We all know and realize that we are accountable to God and will answer to Him someday in the future. We must also understand that we will answer for the way we treated our fellowman. The greatest commandment is to love God with all your heart but the second greatest is to love your neighbor as yourself. We are to submit to each other (Ephesians 5:21). It is at the church that we join the body of Christ and line up side by side as soldiers ready for battle. We answer the call to duty. We can make a difference. We have lined up to be counted. We are counted among the ranks of the redeemed. Every Sunday morning reveille will be sounded. We must get up, get out, and line up for we are called to duty.

There is the **Cause of Compassion**. The church is a place where you can serve. It provides an avenue for you to help others. Most people think that just showing up is a big enough contribution. This is a start but not a goal. There is always more to be done than those who will do it. We are reminded that Christ said the harvest truly is great but the laborers are few (Luke 10:2). The church needs you. You have gifts that are waiting to be unwrapped. You have the answer to someone's question. You possess a smile that someone needs to see. You have a word that needs to be heard. Get plugged in and be a vital part of the church.

There is the **Wonder of Worship**. A place of cooperate worship and praise. I can be a part of something bigger than myself. It is God's house. We gather to worship Him. We can worship Him at home or in the woods but there is something special about those who have the same mind and purpose when they gather together and worship God. What makes the sermon more than a speech and the teaching more than school is the anointing of worship. We are created to worship. When Jesus was just a baby, wise men traveled far to come and worship Him, and wise people still travel every Sunday to church to worship Christ.

Excuse # 2
THEY ONLY WANT YOUR MONEY.

I will readily admit that there are those who have taken advantage of the good nature of God's people. There are pastors and T.V. evangelists who have fleeced the flock. The love of money has become their first priority. These folks fail

50

to realize that God wants us to prosper. God wants you to prosper. He is not out to get your money because He doesn't need it. He owns everything.

> *"The **silver** is mine, and the **gold** is mine,"* *saith the Lord of hosts* (Haggai 2:8).

> **The earth** *is the Lord's, and the fulness thereof; the world, and **they** that dwell therein* (Psalm 24:1).

So, God owns it all and He doesn't need our money, but He actually wants you to prosper. We know that God's Word tells us in 3 John 1:2, "Beloved, I wish above all things that thou mayest prosper and be in health, even as thy soul prospereth." Here it is. He wants us to prosper as our soul prospers. Our soul prospers as we understand His Word. His Word teaches us to give.

> *Give, and it shall be given unto you; good measure, pressed down, and shaken together, and running over, shall men give into your bosom. For with the same measure that ye mete withal it shall be measured to you again* (Luke 6:38).

The church wants you to prosper. Also, God uses what we have to build the Kingdom. He returns back to us abundantly and we give of our increase. God has a plan for His sheep to increase and be able to give and increase again. The plan is called *tithing*. It is returning to God a tenth of our weekly increase. This is another reason to attend church. The church is the storehouse where we deposit our tithe. The rule of tithing was instituted in the Old Testament and there is not any credible evidence that it was ever done away with. Look at the plan as it is laid out in Malachi, chapter 3.

> *Even from the days of your fathers ye are gone away from mine ordinances, and have not kept them. "Return unto me, and I will return unto you," saith the Lord of hosts. But ye said, "Wherein shall we return? Will a man rob God? Yet ye have robbed me." But ye say, "Wherein have we robbed thee?" In **tithes and offerings**. Ye are cursed with a curse: for ye have robbed me, even this whole nation. "Bring ye all the tithes into the **storehouse**, that there may be meat in mine house, and prove me now herewith," saith the Lord of hosts, "if I will not open you the windows of heaven, and **pour you out a blessing**, that there shall not be room enough to receive it. And I will rebuke the devourer for your sakes, and he shall not destroy the fruits of your ground; neither shall your vine cast her fruit before the time in the field," saith the Lord of hosts. "And all nations shall call you blessed: for ye shall be a delightsome land," saith the Lord of hosts (vv. 7-12).*

What a plan! When followed, it benefits the church and the individual immensely. This is yet another benefit of attending church—an opportunity to give.

God's sheep were created to have plenty of wool. It is the shepherd that sheers the sheep. The wool will grow again. If a shepherd doesn't trim the sheep regularly then the sheep's wool will get long and matted with dirt and debris and the sheep will become "cast down." The sheep will become so heavy that it won't be able to get up. Unless the shepherd rescues the sheep, it will die. Any good shepherd will sheer his sheep. You can only skin a sheep once but you can sheer it for life and both will be the better for it.

Excuse # 3
I HAD A BAD EXPERIENCE.

Who hasn't! About everyone I know has been hurt in church at one time or the other. Some will quit and others will continue. Some will give up while others will go on. Some will get bitter and others will get better.

First Timothy 4:1 tells of this truth.

> *Now the Spirit speaketh expressly, that in the latter times some shall depart from the faith, giving heed to seducing spirits . . .*

There will be some who will depart and give heed, but there will be others who will stay and ignore those who tried to hurt them. Just because one person in church hurts you does not mean everyone wants to hurt you. Just because one church wounded you doesn't mean the next church will damage you. If you got sick eating a hamburger would you say, "I got sick once so I'm never going to eat again"? No, you may not eat at the same establishment but you would eat again somewhere soon. There are good churches in your community. Do your research and find one, then attend it regularly. Give it more than a couple of Sundays.

Remember, not anyone who attends church is perfect. Not everyone is even a Christian. The majority are loving and caring born-again Christians. It's been said, "We are not what we should be but we are not what we once were either." D.T. Niles said. "Christianity is one beggar telling another beggar where to find bread."

The ground truly is level at the cross. You have as much right to attend church as anyone else. Don't let someone stand between you and God. Move around the obstacle and get closer to the Savior. Attend church this Sunday.

Excuse # 4
THE CHURCH IS FULL OF HYPOCRITES.

The real hypocrites are in the church. Think about it! If the hypocrites were at home when church was assembled, then they (hypocrites) wouldn't actually be hypocrites, they would be sinners. Someone once said, "It is better to go to church with the hypocrites than to go to hell with the hypocrites." This is good common sense.

There will be goats and sheep in the same fold. The Lord said to let the wheat and the tares grow together. However, at the judgment, the wheat will go in the barn and the tares will be burnt, and the sheep will be on the right side and the goats on the left. There will always be some antagonism to those who will serve the Lord. There will be wolves that will try to enter the flock and wolves in sheep's clothing to deceive.

Hypocrites are a reality and a part of the church, but do not let them have the church and the privilege of keeping you home. It is the Lord's church and when sinners come through the doors they must be greeted by the saints and not by the hypocrites.

Hypocrites and all, there is still something special about the church. I guess you could backslide while attending church but as long as you keep coming back each Sunday or Wednesday night, there is always the chance and opportunity that the Spirit of the Lord will touch you and renewal will take place. The next trip may be when you get your breakthrough. This was Asaph's experience when he was about to slip back because he got his eyes on the prosperity of the wicked. Psalm 73 says,

But as for me, my feet were almost gone; my steps had well nigh slipped. For I was envious at the foolish, when I saw the prosperity of the wicked. For there are no bands in their death: but their strength is firm. They are not in trouble as other men; neither are they plagued like other men. Therefore pride compasseth them about as a chain; violence covereth them as a garment. . . . They set their mouth against the heavens, and their tongue walketh through the earth. Therefore his people return hither: and waters of a full cup are wrung out to them. And they say, How doth God know? and is there knowledge in the most High? Behold, these are the ungodly, who prosper in the world; they increase in riches. . . .When I thought to know this, it was too painful for me;

Until I went into the sanctuary of God; then understood I their end.

It is amazing what one trip to church can do. We need to be reminded on a regular basis about the goodness and greatness of God. God will reward the righteous and punish the wicked. When we attend the house of God things are put back into the proper perspective. The truth is spoken and those who are listening will hear. The legitimate gospel is present and those who are looking will see. The Holy Spirit will be at hand and those who are reaching out will feel Him. The manna of the Word will be on the table and the hungry will eat. The water of life will flow freely and the thirsty will drink. All this and more is available at the church. We must not forsake the assembling of ourselves as some have but assemble more as you see the day of the Lord approaching (Hebrews 10:25).

GOOD HABIT

GO TO BED SATURDAY NIGHT READY TO ATTEND CHURCH ON SUNDAY MORNING.

Many people will get up on Sunday and ask, "Are we going to church today?" Don't ask the question. Don't let that be your routine. Set the Alarm clock the night before. Get up, having already made your mind up, that you are going to church. It's Sunday, this is our custom, and we go to church on Sunday.

Upon the first day of the week let every one of you lay by him in store, as God hath prospered him . . . (1 Corinthans 16:2).

REFLECTION POINTS

1) The importance of attending a church cannot be over emphasized. How has your attendance been lately?

   (a) Great   (d) Poor
   (b) Good   (e) None
   (c) Slack

2) An excuse often used for nonattendance is that I can pray at home. This is good but what are we missing when we are not at church?

   The _____Factor
   The Dynamics of _____
   The Act of _____
   The Cause of _____
   The Wonder of _____

3) God is a giver and we are most like Him when we are givers. He has instituted a plan called tithing. What percent of our income is the tithe?

   (a)   5 percent
   (b) 10 percent
   (c) 20 percent
   (d) 50 percent

4) Many people have had a bad experience at church. If you have, take a moment and pray for those who have offended you. Also pray for God to help you to never be a stumbling block to someone else.

CHAPTER FIVE

HAVE A DAILY TIME OF PRAYER

Prayer is our communication with God and God communicating with us. Prayer is speaking and also listening.

> *Pray alone. Let prayer be the key of the morning and the bolt at night. The best way to fight against sin is to fight it on our knees* (Philip Henry).

The following scripture is vital when it comes to understanding prayer.

> *And when thou prayest, thou shalt not be as the hypocrites are: for they love to pray standing in the synagogues and in the corners of the*

streets, that they may be seen of men. Verily I say unto you, "They have their reward. But thou, when thou prayest, enter into thy closet, and when thou hast shut thy door, pray to thy Father which is in secret; and thy Father which seeth in secret shall reward thee openly. But when ye pray, use not vain repetitions, as the heathen do: for they think that they shall be heard for their much speaking. Be not ye therefore like unto them: for your Father knoweth what things ye have need of, before ye ask him. After this manner therefore pray ye: 'Our Father which art in heaven, Hallowed be thy name. Thy kingdom come. Thy will be done in earth, as it is in heaven. Give us this day our daily bread. And forgive us our debts, as we forgive our debtors. And lead us not into temptation, but deliver us from evil: For thine is the kingdom, and the power, and the glory, for ever. Amen'" (Matthew 6:5-13).

This portion of God's Word contains a wealth of information to help us in our endeavor to learn about prayer. Here, Jesus teaches us in His own words about prayer. We can see the why, the where, the how, how often, and what for.

1. Why do we pray?

Thy Father which seeth in secret shall reward them openly (Matthew 6:6).

Prayer to God is for our benefit. The Bible says in Hebrews 11:6, "for he that cometh to God must believe that he

is, and that he is a **rewarder** of them that diligently seek him."
Our first prayer brought us the reward of salvation. God is our
Father and like any good father, He loves to give gifts to His
children. Like children, we are to ask our Father, this is what
prayer is.

> *If ye then, being evil, know how to give good*
> *gifts unto your children, how much more shall*
> *your Father which is in heaven give good*
> *things to them that ask him? (Matthew 7:11).*

> *Yet ye have not, because ye ask not. Ye ask, and*
> *receive not, because ye ask amiss* (James 4:2-3).

So, why do we pray? The task you will attempt is too
large, the burden you will carry is too heavy and the
assignment you are to do is too great. You cannot do it alone.
We must have God's help. This is why we pray.

When we pray we are in essence demonstrating our belief
in God. Again, Hebrews 11:6 says, *"for he that cometh to God*
must believe." We acknowledge our inabilities and His
capability. We believe that God rewards those who seek Him.
Therefore we pray.

2. Where do we pray?

> *But thou, when thou prayest, enter into thy closet*
> (Matthew 6:6).

What is the closet? Does this scripture refer to a place
where we keep our clothes? The answer is found in the
remainder of the text when it says "and when thou hast shut

thy door, pray to thy Father which is in secret." Therefore, the closet is my secret place of prayer. It is the place where I get away from everything else and talk to my Father. We need that special place.

- Adam and Eve had a place in the garden that they would meet God in the cool of the day.
- Abraham built altars and established special places to meet God.
- Jacob had a special place between Beersheba and Haran called Bethel.
- Moses had a place on the mountain.
- Daniel had a special place in his house where he would open the windows and pray three times a day.
- One of Christ's special places was at the Mount of Olives.
- Christ sent His disciples to a special place called the Upper Room to tarry for the Holy Ghost.

That special place for me is down by the creek. I have a creek at my house and also behind the church. Many times as I approach the prayer place, I can sense God's presence already there waiting on me. Sometimes when I've neglected my prayer time, He says to me, "I've been waiting on you and I have missed you." This is our place. Sometimes I talk and many times I just sit there and listen but every time it makes a difference in my life.

Your special place may be under a tree, down by the creek, on a hill, in the garden or many other places that you can imagine. The important thing is that you have a place that you go to meet God. An altar is where you build it. Build an altar and God will come down.

3. How do we pray?

After this manner therefore pray ye . . .
(Matthew 6:9)

A person is not expected to recite the Lord's Prayer each day. This is given as an example of prayer. This is an outline for a proper prayer to a gracious God. As a matter of fact, we pray from our heart more than with our mind. Prayer is talking to God and listening to Him also. The real value of prayer is not that He will hear us but that we can hear Him. Prayer positions us in a place to hear. So, pray with a listening ear.

4. Who do we pray to?

. . . Our Father which art in heaven,
Hallowed be thy name (v. 9).

We are invited to come boldly before the throne of God; however, we should never take this invitation lightly nor abuse it. He is our heavenly Father, yet His name should be hallowed. This means to set Him apart, sanctify or exalt Him above all things. We must be stricken with awe and admiration for He is a great God. We respect His name; we reverence His spirit and resonate His supremacy throughout the universe with exaltation when we hallow His name. Spend time at the beginning of your prayer to bless the name of God. Sanctify Him and celebrate who He is.

5. What do we pray for?

Thy kingdom come. Thy will be done in earth, as it is in heaven. Give us this day our daily bread. And forgive us our debts, as we forgive our debtors. And lead us not into temptation, but deliver us from evil (vv. 10-13).

These are heartfelt requests. These are daily needs. The sooner God's kingdom appears, the better. His will is needed every day as is daily bread. Forgiveness is an ongoing need in our lives. Let us search our hearts for those that we may need to forgive, and God in turn will forgive us. Temptation is on every front. I need deliverance. What more important needs are there than these?

6. How often do we pray?

. . . Give us this day our daily bread (v. 11).

All the previous prayer needs are immediate. There is plenty to pray for today. Matthew 6:34 says,

Take therefore no thought for the morrow: for the morrow shall take thought for the things of itself. Sufficient unto the day is the evil thereof.

Prayer is a conversation with God so talk to Him regularly. The Scripture refers to this as praying without ceasing. Also, prayer is like a friend calling another and enjoying their time together. Prayer can be a special event to which we attend such as a prayer meeting with other believers. Prayer can be a time of solitude with God. This would be when we enter our prayer closet for that close-up, personal fellowship with our Creator. There are many references in the Scriptures to praying daily. It is hard to walk away from God while you are talking to Him.

> **The main thing is to keep the main thing the main thing, and the main thing is PRAYER**

7. Wherefore do we pray?

> *For thine is the kingdom, and the power, and the glory, for ever. Amen* (Matthew 6:13).

He is in control. He is the source of power. All for His glory. Where else could we go? He alone is worthy and able. He is the Creator; the beginning and the end. He is more than able to do exceedingly and abundantly above all that I can ask.

The main thing is to keep the main thing the main thing, and the main thing is *prayer*. Prayer can be voiced anywhere, everywhere, and at any time. I received an e-mail one day that said something like this:

> In your *happy* moments, PRAISE GOD.
> In those *difficult* moments, SEEK GOD.
> During your *quiet* moments, WORSHIP GOD.
> With those *painful* moments, we must TRUST GOD
> and with *every* moment, we need to THANK GOD

65

Prayer is the link that holds everything together. All throughout the Scripture our victory comes because of prayer. The enemy of our souls knows how important prayer is. He will try to distract you and busy you with good things to keep you from praying. Early in the formation of the church in Acts 6, The apostles were taking care of the church in every way. They were busy with the "daily administrations" of the church and people were being neglected. They saw the problem and quickly fixed the issue. Their solution?

Wherefore, brethren, look ye out among you seven men of honest report, full of the Holy Ghost and wisdom, whom we may appoint over this business. But we will give ourselves continually to prayer, and to the ministry of the Word (Acts 6:3-4).

Most would have considered them lazy and self-centered to not take care of the widows and the business of the church. They appointed others to take care of the business and they would pray. The apostles recognized the ultimate importance of prayer.

What was the result of their decision to put prayer first and foremost in their lives?

And when they had prayed, they laid their hands on them. And the word of God increased; and the number of the disciples multiplied in Jerusalem greatly; and a great company of the priests were obedient to the faith. And Stephen, full of faith and power, did great wonders and miracles among the people (Acts 6:6-8).

Prayer brought increase, disciples multiplied, obedience, wonders and miracles. There is plenty to do after we pray but the first thing is to pave the way with prayer. When we work, we work, and when we pray, God works. Pray.

GOOD HABIT

PRAY FIRST THING IN THE MORNING.

Your mind is fresh. It is nothing like starting the day off right with God. You are giving God the firstfruits of your day.

My voice shalt thou hear in the morning, O Lord; in the morning will I direct my prayer unto thee, and will look up (Psalm 5:3).

Try sharing a glass of juice and piece of toast with the Lord while you talk with Him. Develop that special time and discover your special place where you meet God.

REFLECTION POINTS

1) This chapter is about prayer. We talked of the place of prayer. Do you have a special place where you go to pray? If so, where is it?

2) What we pray for is very important. What are you praying for? Make a list of the top seven things you need from God.
   1. _____
   2. _____
   3. _____
   4. _____
   5. _____
   6. _____
   7. _____

3. Compare your list to the things we are supposed to ask for; found in Matthew 10:6-13.

4) Write down a short prayer to God using the example found in the Lord's Prayer.

CHAPTER SIX

READ YOUR BIBLE

And this is the record that God hath given to us eternal life, and this life is in his Son. He that hath the Son hath life; and he that hath not the Son of God hath not life. **These things have I written unto** *you that believe on the name of the Son of God;* **that ye may know** *that ye have eternal life, and that ye may believe on the name of the Son of God* (1 John 5:11-13).

There is no one thing more important to your Christian success than to read and digest the Word of God. I believe it trumps good works, covenant partners, church attendance, praise, and even prayer. Now, I know that is a drastic statement but if I had to give up all the advantageous tools of God and just kept one, it would be the Word of God. The Scripture says in Psalm 138:2,

> *I will worship toward thy holy temple, and praise thy name for thy lovingkindness and for thy truth: for thou hast magnified thy word above all thy name.*

It is the one thing that is durable and sustainable. You are the closest to God when you are reading the Scripture. Christ is the living Word of God.

The Word of God is written so we can know who the Lord is. It is for our instruction and correction. Like a mirror, we look at it and see who we really are. It has been said, "We read books for information but we read the Bible for transformation." It is more than mere words on paper. It feeds our spiritual man like meat and potatoes feed the physical person. This is the way we grow up in Christ.

There's a well-known legend about two wolves:

> *A Cherokee elder was teaching his children about life. "A fight is going on inside me," he said to them. "It is a terrible fight and it is between two wolves. One is evil–he is anger, envy, sorrow, regret, greed, arrogance, self-pity, guilt, resentment, inferiority, lies, false pride, superiority, and ego." He continued, "The other is good–he is joy, peace, love, hope, serenity, humility, kindness, benevolence, empathy, generosity, truth, compassion, and faith. The same fight is going on inside you–*

and inside every other person, too." The
grandchildren thought about it and after a
minute one of them asked, "Which wolf will
win?" The elder simply replied, "The one you
feed" (Author unknown).

As newborn babes, desire the sincere milk of
the word, that ye may grow thereby (1 Peter
2:2).

If you are a new Christian start your Bible reading in the
New Testament. One of the four Gospels is a great place to
begin. The fundaments of the Christian story and the life of
Christ is the primary subject. This is the beginning of the
Christian journey.

If we have had trouble putting our Christian life together,
maybe, we need to read the instruction manual. The Word of
God is a roadmap and a spiritual compass that will keep us on
the right course. We need it for the whole journey. It is a map
and guide that will lead us to heaven.

As we explore the Scripture we realize that we are called
to understand. We understand the very nature of God. The
Scripture is the revelation of who Christ is. The Scripture is
God's personal letter to us. God gave us His Word. The Bible
says in Isaiah 55:11,

So shall my word be that goeth forth out of my
mouth: it shall not return unto me void, but it
shall accomplish that which I please, and it
shall prosper in the thing whereto I sent it.

Statistics show that the person who is engaged in Scripture four or more times per week is . . .

> 70 percent less likely to gamble.
> 60 percent less likely to be involved in pornography.
> 58 percent less likely to use alcohol.
> 200 percent more likely to be involved in personal Evangelism.

(Center for Bible Engagement)

There is no replacement for the Word. Matthew 4:4 says,

Man shall not live by bread alone, but by every word that proceedeth out of the mouth of God.

Psalm 119:67 says, "Before I was afflicted I went astray: but now have I kept thy word." The same chapter says, "Thy word have I hid in mine heart, that I might not sin against thee" (v. 11). This scripture helps us understand a powerful truth. The Word keeps us from going astray. It is saying, "Before, I went astray but now I keep the Word" (paraphrased). The Word will keep us if we keep it. What about you? Look back to a time in your life when you failed God. Were you a student of the Word of God? Were you hiding it in your heart daily?

In this book, I have purposely put in and emphasized the Scripture as much as possible. When we read the Word, we will be strengthened.

It is important how we approach the Scripture. How do we choose to read the Bible? Here are some helpful hints for a good encounter with the Word of God.

- Purchase a Bible that you can write in. Maybe a wide-margin Bible. Mark each chapter as you read.
- Write down scripture references, observations, and insights in your Bible or get a journal to accompany your reading.
- Underline scriptures that speak to you.
- Circle things and highlight whole passages that are your favorite.
- You may want to follow a Bible reading plan that will take you through the Bible in a year. You can get these pamphlets in numerous places.
- It may help to have a special time to read; morning or evening or maybe at lunch or on break while at work.
- Attend a Bible Study
- Listen to the Word on CDs or some other media; maybe a night when you go to bed or in your car.

Again, make a plan for Bible reading. Remember, if we are not planning for success, we are planning for failure.

Psalm 119:105 says, "Thy word is a lamp unto my feet, and a light unto my path."

The Scripture opens our eyes that we may see clearly. It adds light to our walk with God. It teaches me to **LOOK UP** to God in prayer. It is His Word. Jesus Christ is the scarlet thread that runs through the holy pages. He is the central theme of all scripture.

As we approach such a holy God it causes us to **LOOK DOWN** in humility. A very high price has been paid to bring us this precious Word. It is a humbling thought to realize that the great God of an eternal heaven cared enough about us to establish and send us a letter of love and instruction. When my wife, Pam, and I were dating, we always exchanged little love notes at church. There were no cell phones, no texting, or personal computers for our communication but we had notes. Later when I was alone, I would read the note that Pam had written to me. It would contain her deepest thoughts. It would solidify our relationship together. Reading the Bible is what solidifies our intimate relationship with God. It is His love note to us.

The Scripture also helps us to **LOOK OUT** for impending doom. It warns us of the approaching Apocalypse and the Day of Judgment. We can even get a detailed picture of the coming tribulation time in the Book of Revelation. The Bible teaches us how to recognize our enemy and the traps that he will set for each one of us. The Scripture instructs us to look ahead and be prepared for the coming future. The Bible is a book of warnings.

> *I write not these things to shame you, but as my beloved sons I warn you* (1 Corinthians 4:14).

> *Whom we preach, warning every man, and teaching every man in all wisdom; that we may present every man perfect in Christ Jesus* (Colossians 1:28).

Probably, the most important look is the **LOOK IN**. This Word speaks to me first. The beam must be removed from my eye first before I can help remove the mote from someone else's eye (Luke 6:41). When we read the Bible, there is the tendency to focus on someone we know that needs to hear this, and we can't wait to tell what God wants *them* to hear.

74

We must first look at *ourselves*. We have engaged the Word and we are ready for instruction. Allow the Scripture to change you. We do not search the Scriptures to justify our convictions, but rather, let the Word convict us. God will speak into our lives, so we must look deep inside for that divine moment with our Savior as He speaks to us. The Word of God will never change or pass away. It is *we* who must change.

Now, **LOOK AROUND**. Now that I have let the Word do a work on me, I can look to help others. Where does the Scripture instruct me to go? What am I to do? To whom am I to speak? The Scripture is the active Word of God. It challenges us to move forward in our faith. To act on what we have read. Surely, we are our "Brother's Keeper." When we read the story of the Good Samaritan, we watch for the opportunity to become that person in our real life. This is discipleship—learning and then doing.

GOOD HABIT

HAVE A TIME EACH DAY TO READ YOUR BIBLE.

Study to shew thyself approved unto God, a workman that needeth not to be ashamed, rightly dividing the word of truth **(Timothy 2:15).**

Keep a journal where you can record your thoughts as you explore God's Word.

REFLECTION POINTS

1) The Bible is the Word of God. Do you have a good study Bible? ___ yes ___ no

Note: I recommend a King James Version Bible with center reference and a wide margin to write your notes in. This is a great Bible. The KJV has been around for 400 years. It is tried and proved.

2) According to the Center for Bible Engagement, a person that reads the Bible at least four times a week is . . .

____% less likely to gamble.
____% less likely to be involved in pornography.
____% less likely to use alcohol.
____% more likely to be involved in personal evangelism.

3) Matthew 4:4 says, "But he answered and said, 'It is written, Man shall not live by _____ alone, but by every _____ that proceedeth out of the mouth of God.'"

4) Psalm 119:105 says, "Thy word is a_____ unto my feet, and a _____ unto my path."

CHAPTER SEVEN

SEPARATE YOURSELF FROM YOUR OLD LIFE

Therefore if any man be in Christ, he is a new creature: old things are passed away; behold, all things are become new (2 Corinthians 5:17).

The premise *born again* indicates to new believers that they have received a new start. The Scripture says in 2 Corinthians 5: that we are a new creature in Christ. We have a new life. All things have become new. We have crossed the bridge of mercy and grace that was built by our Savior. Now that we have a new life, we are encouraged to move forward. Second Corinthians 6:17 says, "Wherefore come out from among them, and be ye separate," saith the

Lord, "and touch not the unclean thing; and I will receive you."

The first call as a Christian is to COME UNTO CHRIST.

Come unto me, all ye that labour and are heavy laden, and I will give you rest (Matthew 11:28).

The call goes out to the tired and the weary. Christ takes all. You don't have to have treasure or talent to get noticed or invited. If you will come and follow Him, He will give you rest. What a promise!

The reason some people never experience the rest is because they remain torn in their commitment. Some tend to teeter-totter back and forth between coming and going. We are in and out of church, up and down in our walk, back and forth in our commitment, and we develop a wishy-washy mentality concerning the things of Christ. There is no wonder that we have no rest. We are here one minute and there another. The first step is total dependence on Christ. Burn your bridges that are behind. We must have a *no retreat* and *no surrender* attitude. This must be my final answer. When I look at the hand that God dealt me, *I am all in*.

Secondly, to come to Christ means we MUST COME OUT FROM AMONG THEM who oppose Him. As we come to Christ He promises peace. He gives us real life and gives us life more abundantly. Nothing will pull us down faster than trying to take hold of Christ's hand without letting go of the world.

There is a temptation to glamorize our old past life. When we turn our thoughts back to our old life, we are flirting with disaster. The old friends, the old places, and the old pastimes will pull us away from the Lord if we allow it. There is a true saying, "The company you keep determines the trouble you meet." A parrot got loose and flew into the cornfield with the crows. When the farmer began to shoot crows, the parrot was wounded. While picking up dead crows, he saw the wounded parrot and picked it up. The parrot began to speak, "Bad company! Bad company! This was the case with Lot and his encounter with Sodom and Gomorrah. Lot was under the tutelage of his uncle Abraham. He did well while he was with Abraham. They both prospered so much that the land could not hold them. They separated and Abraham gave Lot his choice as to which direction that he would go. We see him make the wrong choice in Genesis 13:10-12. "And Lot lifted up his eyes, and beheld all the plain of Jordan, that it was well watered everywhere, before the Lord destroyed Sodom and Gomorrah, even as the garden of the Lord, like the land of Egypt, as thou comest unto Zoar. Then Lot chose him all the plain of Jordan; and Lot journeyed east, and they separated themselves the one from the other. Abram dwelled in the land of Canaan, and Lot dwelled in the cities of the plain, and pitched his tent toward Sodom."

The power of influence is a commanding thing. You can take a righteous man and put him among the wicked and over time it will vex his spirit. Lot pitched his tent toward Sodom. Every day it drew him a little closer and the influence of the evil made a difference in his life.

Be ye not unequally yoked together with unbelievers: for what fellowship hath righteousness with unrighteousness? and what communion hath light with darkness? (2 Corinthians 6:14).

How many folks have jumped in the car with someone and thought they were just going to ride around for awhile only to find out they were included in a criminal act such as a holdup, drug activity, etc., and then were caught by the police. This happens and many times the innocent person will be judged guilty and penalized like they were voluntarily involved.

Maybe someone went with a friend that they knew was a troublemaker and against their better judgment did it anyway, only to find themselves in a fight because of the company they kept.

Before the separation from Abraham, Lot was a very wealthy and prosperous individual. It didn't take long until he lost it all. The company he kept at Sodom and Gomorrah zapped what little blessing he still possessed. Second Peter 2:7-8 says,

Lot, vexed with the filthy conversation of the wicked: (For that righteous man dwelling among them, in seeing and hearing, vexed his righteous soul from day to day with their unlawful deeds)

Dwelling among them can cancel your blessing. The scripture says in seeing and hearing Lot was vexed. What you

80

look at, what you listen to, where you go, and who you go with makes a difference!

After Lot was separated from the godly influence of his uncle Abraham he associated himself with the ungodly in Sodom and Gomorrah.

As a growing, living new creature in Christ, it is important what you digest spiritually. What you hear, see, and experience will determine how you progress in your growth process. There is a little Sunday school song that says,

> O be careful little eyes what you see.
> O be careful little ears what you hear.
> O be careful little feet where you go.

In the chorus, we are reminded that the Father up above is looking down in love so we need to be careful.

> Be careful what you look at.
> Be careful what you listen to.
> Be careful where you go.
> Be careful who you go with.

You know the old story of how to boil a frog. You don't put him in a pot of boiling water. You drop him in the boiling water and he will jump out before he is injured. So, you put him in a pot of cool water, and he's perfectly comfortable. Then you put him on the stove, and little by little, the water gets warm. It is very pleasant at first. Then it gets to Jacuzzi level, and he begins to be a little alarmed. Finally, when it is boiling, it is too late. Some Christians are like that. They try to live as close to the world as possible. First, they get into the world and it's oh so pleasant—at first. And then it gets a little warmer and it's better yet. And one day they realize the danger: **This is going to kill me.** Only to recognize, **I am already done for.**

Many times we fail to burn the bridges of our old life and it becomes all too easy for us to return. There are many strong references to the ultimate destruction of the "old person" that we were before salvation. We have a new life and we are to be dead to the old one. Look at the following scriptures:

> *Knowing this, that our old man is crucified with him, that the body of sin might be destroyed, that henceforth we should not serve sin* (Romans 6:6).

> *And they that are Christ's have crucified the flesh with the affections and lusts* (Galatians 5:24).

> *I am crucified with Christ: nevertheless I live; yet not I, but Christ liveth in me: and the life which I now live in the flesh I live by the faith of the Son of God, who loved me, and gave himself for me* (Galatians 2:20).

Thirdly, we need to COME INTO OUR NEW FAMILY. God will not ask us to cast off all our old acquaintances, old hangouts, and old stuff without replacing them with positive people, proper places, and terrific things that will help to develop us into what God wants us to be.

The easy path is very seldom the best choice. The Bible warns that there is a broad way with a wide gate that leads to destruction and many go that way. There is a straight and narrow way that leads to eternal life and there is only a few that find it (Matthew 7:13-14). This does not mean that it is hard to live for God. Matter of fact, the Bible says in Proverbs 13:15, "Good understanding giveth favour: but the way of transgressors is hard." What the scripture means is that anyone can stumble their way into hell, but the steps toward heaven will be intentional and on purpose.

It will take effort on your part to power up the positive. We are surrounded by the negative. The modern media makes a living selling the negative. Something good can happen across the street and it may be next month before you hear about it. On the other hand, something negative and bad happens on the other side of the world and it will make the 6 o'clock news, the next day's newspaper, and someone will write a book or make a movie. The help you need to be positive will only come from other positive people. You will reap huge benefits from the influence of a positive environment.

Surround yourself with a positive environment:

- People that build you.
- Places that lift you.
- Things that help you.
- Thoughts that inspire you.

We need to keep company with those who build up our relationship with God and add to our faith, not tear them down. If we seek first the kingdom of God …all these things

83

will be added unto us. "Seek ye first the kingdom" (Matthew 6:33). Follow closely to God. Instead of trying to get away with as much as possible, we need to get as close as possible.

The apostle Peter denied the Lord three times. This is the worst possible sin. When the crowd came to the garden to take Christ away, Peter rose up to challenged them and cut off the High Priest's servant's ear. Peter was a bold, strong man. He was full of adventure. He even tried to walk on water one time. He was a fisherman who rowed boats and threw heavy nets. He was not afraid. He was standing tall and full of passion. When the mob left with Christ held captive, Peter's passion dwindled. He followed but it was at a distance. Look at the text.

> *Then took they him, and led him, and brought him into the high priest's house. And Peter **followed afar off**. And when they had kindled a fire in the midst of the hall, and were set down together, **Peter sat down among them**. But a certain maid beheld him as he sat by the fire, and earnestly looked upon him, and said, "this man was also with him"* (Luke 22:54-56).

He followed at a distance. He then warmed himself at the fire of the enemy. They immediately recognized that he was out of place. He was recognized as one of the disciples.

You may follow at a distance and try to cozy up to the fire of this world, but it will never be like it was when you were a sinner. The drink will never again taste good. The sin will not be as enjoyable or the party any fun. You have tasted of the goodness of the Lord and the old life will never have the same

84

appeal. Sin at its best is only enjoyable for a short season. The good news is that Christ brings true joy to the table. The worst day as a Christian is better than the best day as an infidel. Psalm 84:10 says it best, "For a day in thy courts is better than a thousand. I had rather be a doorkeeper in the house of my God, than to dwell in the tents of wickedness."

Let God do a new work in you. The road is straight and narrow but it is a wonderful journey.

GOOD HABIT

HANG OUT AND FELLOWSHIP WITH CHRISTIANS.

Join a small group at church.
Attend every fellowship function.
Go on a church outing.
Facebook with Christian friends

And have no fellowship with the unfruitful works of darkness, but rather reprove them (Ephesians 5:11).

REFLECTION POINTS

1) This chapter is about separation from the old life. What was in your old life that tried to pull you back? List three things that you struggle with and make them top priority in your prayer time.

    a)

    b)

    c)

2) The scripture says, "Come out from among them." We talked about the "what" in question 1, now it is the "who." When you are around some people they pull you down and speak negative things into your life. There may be someone that you need to separate yourself from. Who is it? (Don't write name.)

3) On the other hand there are those who build you up and encourage you. List three people that are a positive influence in your life.

    a)

    b)

    c)

    Maybe you could send them a card this week and let them know that you appreciate them.

CHAPTER EIGHT

DISCERN THE DIFFERENCE BETWEEN TEMPTATION AND TRIBULATION

These are two words that look alike and even sound familiar. One is an instrument of destruction while the other is a tool for construction. Temptation is an occasion to fail while tribulation is an opportunity to succeed. When we encounter temptation, we need to escape. During tribulation we need to endure. We need to learn to recognize the difference. Every struggle in life needs not be avoided. Temptation comes from the heart of Satan to destroy our relationship with God. While tribulation may channel through the devil, its primary purpose is to strengthen our walk with God. Temptation is the devil's "hidden trap" but tribulation is an "out-in-the open" fight.

THE TEMPTATION OF ADAM AND EVE

Temptation is not a sin in itself but it is the devil's enticement to sin. Most of the time it begins in the mind and is planted in our thought processes and takes root long before it reaches the fruit of sin.

A close look at the first temptation recorded in the Scripture reveals the true nature of the devil and the enticement of sin. In Genesis 3, God created man and placed Adam and Eve in the garden of God to tend it. God would come by in the cool of the day to visit. It was a perfect place where all their needs were met. Then the devil entered and challenged the relationship and enticed Adam and Eve to fall from the grace of God. Let's look at the scripture.

> *Now the serpent was more subtil than any beast of the field which the Lord God had made. And he said unto the woman, "**Yea,**" hath God said, "Ye shall not eat of every tree of the garden?" And the woman said unto the serpent, "We may eat of the fruit of the trees of the garden: But of the fruit of the tree which is in the midst of the garden, God hath said, 'Ye shall not eat of it, neither shall ye touch it, lest ye die.'" And the serpent said unto the woman, "**Ye shall not surely die:** For God doth know that in the day ye eat thereof, then your eyes shall be opened, and ye shall be as gods, knowing good and evil." And when the woman saw that the tree was good for food, and that it was pleasant to the eyes, and a tree to be desired to make one wise, she took of the fruit thereof, and did eat,*

and gave also unto her husband with her; and he did eat. And the eyes of them both were opened, and they knew that they were naked; and they sewed fig leaves together, and made themselves aprons. And they heard the voice of the Lord God walking in the garden in the cool of the day: and Adam and his wife hid themselves from the presence of the Lord God amongst the trees of the garden. And the Lord God called unto Adam, and said unto him, "Where art thou?" (Genesis 3:1-9).

The first thing is that during temptation the devil will always challenge God's Word ". . .Yea, hath God said . . ." God didn't really mean that or it was for someone else. This is the reason that we need to know the Scriptures. We cannot get too much of the Word into our lives. David said in Psalm 119:11, "Thy word have I hid in mine heart, that I might not sin against thee."

When Jesus was tempted at the beginning of His earthly ministry, Satan again challenged the Word of God. In Matthew 4, the Lord had fasted 40 days and was hungry. Satan tried to take advantage of Christ's hunger and tempt Him to turn rocks into bread. The Lord said, "Man shall not live by bread alone . . ." He quoted the Word. Then the devil quoted the scripture himself. He will deceive by misquoting and taking scripture out of context. He is really challenging the validity of the Bible. Like Christ, we must know the scriptures. We commit error because we do not know the scriptures. When we hear the enemy say, "hath God said" we need to know if He said it or not (Mark 12:24).

The second thing the devil does consistently is lie. He is a liar and the father of lies (John 8:44). He told Eve that she would not die if she ate the forbidden fruit (Genesis 3:4). He lied. She would die and did. She and her husband, Adam, died spiritually the moment she yielded to temptation. They fell out of fellowship with God. Also, they begin to die physically from that moment forward. They were to live forever in the garden. The devil lied to them. He is not constrained to tell the truth. He will lie to you. He came to Eve in the form of a serpent which was very cunning and crafty. He will come to tempt you through someone else. He never shows up in a red suit with a pitchfork in his hand. He will appear as an angel of light to deceive you. He works through people that you feel comfortable around. He challenges the truth of God and he is a liar. Be on guard. Lean on the truth of God. It never changes and it will support you when your faith is tested.

So, how do we deal with temptation? It is everywhere. We are bombarded on every side with opportunities to sin. It speaks "sweet nothings" in our ears by way of the airways. Neon signs flash in our faces. It sets up shop in our living rooms and spins its web. It calls to us from the darkness to come a little closer, make more money, have more fun, live the high life, go for the gusto; in other words, give up, give in, and sell your soul. What can we do? How do we combat temptation?

1. PRAY

There are many things we can do after we pray but none so important as to pray. We come to God for guidance. We pray, "Lead us in a path that will avoid the temptation." We come to God for strength. "Lord help us overcome the fleshly desires and our worldly wishes." We also become conscious of the fact that temptation is farthest from us when we are closest to God.

> *Watch and pray, that ye enter not into temptation: the spirit indeed is willing, but the flesh is weak* (Matthew 26:41).

> *And when he was at the place, he said unto them, "Pray that ye enter not into temptation"* (Luke 22:40).

> *And said unto them, "Why sleep ye? rise and pray, lest ye enter into temptation"* (Luke 22:46).

> *And forgive us our sins; for we also forgive every one that is indebted to us. And lead us not into temptation; but deliver us from evil* (Luke 11:4).

2. GET INTO THE WORD

> *. . . The seed is the word of God. Those by the way side are they that hear; then cometh the devil, and taketh away the word out of their hearts, lest they should believe and be saved. They on the rock are they, which, when they hear, receive the word with joy; and these have no root, which for a while believe, and in time of temptation fall away. And that which fell among thorns are they, which, when they have heard, go forth, and are choked with cares and riches and pleasures of this life, and bring no fruit to perfection* (Luke 8:11-14).

The devil hates the Word of God so much that when it is sown into our lives, he will immediately try to steal it from us. When this doesn't work, he entangles it with thorns or undermines it with stones to make it ineffective. If we have not taken root in the things of God, the enemy of our souls will turn up the heat of temptation and we will fail. Let the Word have the good ground of your heart. Nurture it and let it grow deep into your soul and spirit. You will grow strong and produce fruit for the kingdom of God. Over and over again, the two most important disciplines of the Christian are to PRAY and STUDY the Scriptures.

3. LOOK FOR THE ESCAPE

God hasn't saved you to fail. He hasn't picked you up out of the mire of sin to cast you back down. He wants you to succeed. When the devil has a plan to take you out, God has a plan that will keep you in. When temptation comes your way, it hasn't taken God by surprise. He has an escape plan. Look for it. The devil has come to steal, kill, and destroy, but God has come to give you abundant life. He is faithful. He will never fail us. When up against the Red Sea and Pharaoh's army has blocked our path, God has a plan. When we can't go left, right, or even back up, God has a plan. When we don't have a boat to float us across or seemly no way of escape from the enemy, God has a plan. He makes a way where there is no way. God has a plan.

> *There hath no temptation taken you but such as*
> *is common to man: but God is faithful, who will*
> *not suffer you to be tempted above that ye are*
> *able; but will with the temptation also make a*

way to escape, that ye may be able to bear it (1 Corinthians 10:13).

THE TRIBULATION OF THE SAINTS

Do you remember the moment that you were born again? I do. There was such joy in my heart and a freshness in my soul that occurred. We tend to take a deep breath, let it out in relief, and think the past is behind, that there is no rain in sight and the road ahead is smooth. We set the vehicle on cruise control, adjust the seat to a comfortable position, and get ready to enjoy the ride. Then we are sideswiped, we spin out of control, and are knocked off that road. We awake in a stunned stupor and wonder what just happened. It is called TRIBULATION.

After the crash, you find yourself upright, and amazingly enough, the car started again, and it is still drivable. It is a little beat up with some broken glass, but it will get us to the destination just fine. You will proceed with a lot more caution and a little more driving experience in hopes of avoiding future encounters.

DON'T QUIT!
IT'S JUST A BUMP IN THE ROAD!
IT IS NOT THE END OF THE ROAD!

Tribulation is a part of the Christian journey. As long as we are in this world we will have tribulation. Tribulation will cause some to stray while it will make others strong.

WE ARE TO EXPECT TROUBLE.

Beloved, think it not strange concerning the fiery trial which is to try you, as though some strange thing happened unto you (1 Peter 4:12).

WE ARE TO HAVE JOY IN THE MIDST OF TROUBLE.

But rejoice, inasmuch as ye are partakers of Christ's sufferings; that, when his glory shall be revealed, ye may be glad also with exceeding joy. If ye be reproached for the name of Christ, happy are ye; for the spirit of glory and of God resteth upon you: on their part he is evil spoken of, but on your part he is glorified (vv. 13, 14).

YOU MAY BE IN TROUBLE BECAUSE YOU HAVE DONE WRONG.

But let none of you suffer as a murderer, or as a thief, or as an evildoer, or as a busybody in other men's matters (v.15).

YOU MAY BE IN TROUBLE BECAUSE YOU HAVE DONE RIGHT.

Yet if any man suffer as a Christian, let him not be ashamed; but let him glorify God on this behalf (v.16).

When you are in trouble, it is important to try to understand why and where it is coming from. It may be something that you can do to ease your own suffering. I may need to avoid something or someone. My environment may be my demise. I may need to endure. In the Bible there are different situations and reasons for trouble that are found throughout its pages. I will address four of these with a brief description.

THE FIRST IS **NOAH'S TROUBLE.**

Noah was in trouble because he lived in a wicked time. The Scripture says in Genesis 6:5 concerning the time, that, "the wickedness of man was great in the earth, and that every imagination of the thoughts of his heart was only evil continually" Much like today, evil was on every corner. Mankind constantly dreams up and finds new ways to sin against God.

Noah was God's chosen person to stand for Him in a world that was against Him. Some people will make trouble for you just because you are a Christian. They don't really know you but they are against you. It is not you but what and who you stand for. This world is antichrist. It hated Christ and it will hate us because of Christ. Christ reminded us that we are in this world and for that reason we will have tribulation, but we are not to let that get us down because He overcame the world (John 16:33).

In 2 Timothy, Paul warns Timothy of an evil man named Alexander who had done him much evil. He said the Lord would take care of Alexander and reward him for his evil. There were Jannes and Jambres, Pharaoh's magicians, who withstood Moses and came against the work of God (2 Timothy 4:14). We are surrounded by evil and live in an atheistic, liberal, God-hating society; we are insulated by the spirit of God. We shall overcome. This is not our home. We are aliens here and will never be accepted. Christ is preparing a place for all those who love Him, and just like Noah, we shall be delivered. The water that destroyed the world was the instrument that floated the ark to safety

> *And spared not the old world, but saved Noah the eighth person, a preacher of righteousness, bringing in the flood upon the world of the ungodly* (2 Peter 2:5).

THE SECOND IS **PILATES TROUBLE.**

> *He hath shewed thee, O man, what is good; and what doth the Lord require of thee, but to do justly, and to love mercy, and to walk humbly with thy God?*
> (Micah 6:8).

Pontius Pilate served in the high position of governor and desired to please the people. Pilate was caught in the middle and his trouble was his position, which was his job. He knew Christ was no harm to the people. He asked, "What wrong has He done?" He wanted to release Him. He tried to get the Jews to judge Him. His wife was warned in a dream to let Christ go. Pilate even said that he found no fault in Christ at all. He washed his hands of guilt and did what was wrong; he desired to keep his position. Mark 15:15 tells the story, "And so Pilate, willing to content the people, released Barabbas unto them, and delivered Jesus, when he had scourged him, to be crucified."

How sad this is. Many today hope to serve and live for the Lord when they acquire a job or position that pleases God. They say, "When I get straightened out, I'll come to church." What we are saying is, "My position will not allow me to do what is right." I know people who want to be Christians but discover that they find themselves in the same situation Pilate was in. They are unwilling to give up a business that is ungodly or they are living in sin, unmarried, because they will lose government assistance if they do what is right.

You may find yourself in a job or position in which you are required to cheat, lie, or do something that you know is wrong. Possibly, you will be asked to go with the majority or play along with the seniority. These are struggles that we can easily find ourselves in. What are we to do? We must pray and let the Holy Spirit lead us. Pray as the Lord taught us in Matthew 6:13, "And lead us not into temptation, but deliver us from evil: For thine is the kingdom, and the power, and the glory, for ever. Amen."

To please God should be our utmost desire, and this, friend, will cause you some trouble. To do what is right is seldom easy but always necessary. It was George Washington who said, "Few men have the virtue to withstand the highest bidder." Robert E. Lee said, "You have only always to do what is right. It will become easier by practice, and you will enjoy in the midst of your trials the pleasure of an approving conscience."

THIRD, THERE IS **JOB'S TROUBLE**

Job was the blessed, wealthy, God-fearing, sin-hating man of his day. We read in the first chapter of Job how he lost it

98

all. The oxen and the donkeys were stolen by the Sabeans, and they killed the servants. Fire fell from heaven and burned up the sheep and their caretakers. The Chaldeans took the camels and killed the servants. A whirlwind came through the wilderness and destroyed the house, where Job's sons and daughters were having a party, and killed them. In each instance only one servant survived to bring the devastating news to Job. In a matter of minutes all 7,000 sheep, 500 oxen, 500 donkeys, 3,000 camels, and all but four servants and his 10 children were gone.

Some say the devil was out to get Job. I think the devil is out to get all of us, but the main focus for Job in this story is not the devil but God. It was God who suggested that the devil take a look at Job.

And the Lord said unto Satan, "Hast thou considered my servant Job, that there is none like him in the earth, perfect and an upright man, one that feareth God, and escheweth evil? (Job 1:8).

The devil had not even mentioned Job, but it was God's suggestion to consider Job as a target of persecution. We tend to blame the devil for all our problems, when in fact; every tribulation has to come across the "desk" of God in order for Him to sign off on the trial. With Job the order originates on the "desk" of God.

This is somewhat hard to grasp, but when this is the case, it is important that we recognize it quickly. God has allowed this tribulation to come our way to give us an opportunity to increase if we pass the test. We don't need a way out, we need to endure to the end. The end in Job's case was twice as many camels, oxen, sheep and donkeys. He had seven more sons and three more daughters that were the fairest in the land.

When we realize that God has brought us into our trouble we must handle the situation like Job did. As quick as the bad news came, Job made the right move.

> *Then Job arose, and rent his mantle, and shaved his head, and fell down upon the ground, and worshipped, And said, "Naked came I out of my mother's womb, and naked shall I return thither: the Lord gave, and the Lord hath taken away; blessed be the name of the Lord." In all this Job sinned not, nor charged God foolishly (Job 1:20-22).*

Job didn't say that it was not God's fault; matter of fact, he said that "God gives and He takes away," but the scripture said that he did not charge God foolishly. God knows what He is doing. We must accept that He is in control. We should not lay anything to His charge. He has a plan. Psalm 66 reminds us of the plan of God when He leads us into trouble. He has a destination in mind. Look at a portion of this psalm.

> *For thou, O God, hast proved us: thou hast tried us, as silver is tried Thou broughtest us into the net; thou laidst affliction upon our loins. Thou hast caused men to ride over our heads; we went through fire and through water: but thou broughtest us out into a wealthy place (Psalm 66:10-12).*

It was God that tried us. He led us to the net, put affliction upon us, caused others to get ahead of us, and sent us through fire and flood. Why? He was bringing us to a WEALTHY PLACE. It was a process to bless us. Romans 8:28 says, "And we know that all things work together for good to them that love God, to them who are the called according to his purpose."

Have you ever heard of **THE PATIENCE OF JOB**?

> *My brethren, count it all joy when ye fall into divers temptations; Knowing this, that the trying of your faith worketh patience. But let patience have her perfect work, that ye may be perfect and entire, wanting nothing* (James 1:2-4).

Job let patience have her perfect work. Job 42:16-17 says, "After this lived Job an hundred and forty years, and saw his sons, and his sons' sons, even four generations. So Job died, being old and full of days." He went through a trial but endured and lived 140 full, happy years after. God always has our best interest in mind.

FINALLY, THERE IS **JONAH'S TROUBLE.**

> *Now the word of the Lord came unto Jonah the son of Amittai, saying, "Arise, go to Nineveh, that great city, and cry against it; for their wickedness is come up before me." But Jonah rose up to flee . . .* (Jonah 1:1-3).

Most people have heard the story of Jonah and the whale. The problem is summed up in the opening verses of the Book of Jonah. God tells Jonah what to do, where to go, and the reason why, in one sentence. That is far more information than should have been required. Then the scripture says, "But Jonah rose up to flee . . ." He ran the other way in direct disobedience to the call of God.

God has a plan for our lives. He has ordered our steps (Psalm 37:23). His thoughts toward us are good and not evil, in order for us to have hope and good future (Jeremiah 29:11). Sometimes we have a tendency to stray from God's plan and then there may be times of direct disobedience. God loves us too much to let us continue in a wrong direction. He will intervene in the affairs of His children. One of the first things I try to do when I am going through a troubled time is to determine if I have stepped out of the will of God. I seek Him in prayer and search my soul and my actions to determine if I have wandered off course. If I establish that I have missed the mark then I repent and get back on course. The longer you ride the ship of disobedience, the farther out to sea you will travel and the stronger the storm will become.

> *But the Lord sent out a great wind into the sea, and there was a mighty tempest in the sea, so that the ship was like to be broken. Then the mariners were afraid . . .* (Jonah 1:4-5).

Not only will the storm grow stronger but your disobedience can endanger others. There were others on the ship. A disobedient Father can affect the whole family. A disobedient pastor can have an ominous effect on the whole

102

church. A disobedient boss will influence the whole company. This is the worst kind of trouble. You can't afford to be in disobedience or hang around those who are, because when the lightning strikes it may jump over to get you if you are too close. And it will strike.

So if we are suffering, like **Noah**, because of a wicked world then live on and do what is right. In the end you will be delivered. If you are in a dilemma because of your official capacity, such as an appointment or a job, like **Pilate**, then go get another one. Retire or quit. Anything is better than crucifying Christ. Don't give up your destiny with God for a dollar in the world. Do not give away your heavenly future for a moment of fame. It is not worth whatever they are paying you. If by chance you are singled out by God to be tried like **Job**, then when the devil shows up, rejoice and hang on. God believes in you and you must believe in Him. The moment will be devastating, but the future will be bright. When **Jonah** is your name or your companion, the quicker you repent the less the pain will be. Go ahead and be obedient. Isaiah 1:19 says. "If ye be willing and obedient, ye shall eat the good of the land"

GOOD HABIT

PRAY DAILY AND ASK GOD TO DETOUR
TEMPTATION AND HELP YOU
ENDURE TRIBULATION.

And lead us not into temptation, but deliver us from evil: For thine is the kingdom, and the power, and the glory, for ever. Amen (Matthew 6:13).

Sin hinders prayer but prayer hinders sin.

REFLECTION POINTS

1) We understand that temptation is the enemy trying to cause us to fail God. Have you been tempted lately? Did you see the temptation coming? Did you recognize the way of escape that God had for you? Write any thought that you have.

2) Tribulation is God giving us opportunity for success. What is a tribulation that you have encountered lately? Was any of the following involved in the problem? Circle any that apply.

    My Job − A Sinner − A Relationship − Money

    Disobedience − Hostility − I was expected to
    ignore a wrong − Someone expected me to lie.

    Sin − Ridicule − Embarrassment − My Faith

3) Which one of the troubles that we discussed did your problem fall under? (A) Noah's Trouble. (B) Pilate's Trouble. (C) Job's Trouble. (D) Jonah's Trouble.

4) We need to (escape/endure) temptation.

5) We need to (escape/endure) tribulation

CHAPTER NINE

REALIZE THAT YOU WERE SAVED TO GIVE NOT JUST RECEIVE.

That every one of you should know how to possess his vessel in sanctification and honour (1 Thessalonians 4:4).

We are the vessels of God. A vessel is intended to hold something. It is a vessel for reception. We hold and are filled with the spirit of our God. Also, a vessel is intended to disperse its contents. Something is poured in and something is poured out. This makes the vessel useful for its designed purpose. We are to be receivers and givers.

Just south of Israel is the Dead Sea. It has one of the highest concentrations of salt and mineral content in the world. Water flows into it from the Jordan River, but the Dead Sea has no outlet. Since there is no outlet the salt content is so high that life cannot be sustained in the water. Even though it is fed by the fresh, living water of the Jordan, it gives no life. This can be true with us also. Even though the good and fresh flows into our lives, we are dead if it doesn't flow through us. We must let the freshness of God flow through us. He will get to us what He can get through us.

A Christian, who only receives and never gives, is like the Dead Sea. They have received the life of Christ as the fresh river flows in; however, it doesn't sustain life around us because it doesn't flow through us.

GIVING IS GOOD FOR OTHERS.

> *Bring ye all the tithes into the storehouse, that there may be meat in mine house . . .* (Malachi 3:10).

Sometimes, we think what we do does not make a difference. When you give of your treasure to the church, a portion will most likely be put toward helping others. God's house becomes a storehouse for the hungry.

There is a story of a man and woman walking along the beach. They notice that there are thousands of starfish which have been washed in by the tide and left stranded on the beach. The sun is coming up, the tide is going down and the starfish are sure to die.

After they had walked a mile or so, they see a man throwing the starfish, one by one, back into the ocean. The couple knows that he cannot save them all. They called out to him, "You have miles to go, what you are doing will not matter." Holding up a starfish he said, "It matters to this one"

One at a time, we can make a difference. Don't become overwhelmed by the many. God gave you special gifts and talents to rescue a few souls. What you do will matter to the one you help lead to Christ.

GIVING IS GOOD FOR YOU.

> *"Bring ye all the tithes into the storehouse, that there may be meat in mine house, and prove me now herewith," saith the Lord of hosts, "if I will not open you the windows of heaven, and pour you out a blessing, that there shall not be room enough to receive it"* (Malachi 3:10).

Tithing means tenth or ten percent. Tithing is God's plan to bless you. The scripture asks us to prove God and watch Him open the windows of heaven and pour out to us more than we can receive. This is a program to give your treasure.

You can give your time also. When we are working or busy giving we will not have as much time to look for reasons to be unhappy. The man or woman who is on the front lines of a war is usually busy dodging bullets. Small things are not as important as they were when you were at the base camp drinking coffee. Likewise, when we are helping others, our problems don't seem to be as dreadful.

The Bible says that we reap what we sow (Galatians 6:7). We all like a harvest and our harvest is determined when we sow. What you give will be what you receive. The difference is the amount of the item. God will give back abundantly more than we will ever give out.

> *Give, and it shall be given unto you; good measure, pressed down, and shaken together, and running over, shall men give into your bosom. For with the same measure that ye mete withal it shall be measured to you again* (Luke 6:38).

So, giving of both time and treasure is good for you because it gives you a return and it keeps you occupied and your mind on others instead of yourself. Even though it is not in the Bible, Grandma was right when she said, "Idle hands are the devil's workshop."

GIVING IS A BLOW AGAINST THE ENEMY.

> *"And I will rebuke the devourer for your sakes, and he shall not destroy the fruits of your ground; neither shall your vine cast her fruit before the time in the field," saith the Lord of hosts* (Malachi 3:1).

When we give, God rebukes the devil. I can rebuke the enemy when he tries to tempt me. Here, God rebukes him for me, and my giving is what prompts the rebuke.

GIVING IS GOOD FOR THE KINGDOM.

"And all nations shall call you blessed: for ye shall be a delightsome land," saith the Lord of hosts (Malachi 3:12).

Again the Dead Sea is full of salt. It holds this high salt concentration within its banks because of no outlet. This salt kills the life in the sea. To live a fulfilling life, we cannot withhold all the salt, we must influence the world with it. The Lord has great expectations for you. He says in John 14:12, "He that believeth on me, the works that I do shall he do also; and greater works than these shall he do; because I go unto my Father."

"Ye are the salt of the earth . . ." (Matthew 5:13). As we give of ourselves, the salt in us brings healing and preservation to those with whom we come in contact.

God has given us gifts and talents. We have time and treasure to give also. We need to open our gifts and our pockets and find some time to do what we can for the kingdom of God.

GOOD HABIT

BE PREPARED TO GIVE BEFORE YOU GET TO CHURCH

Don't wait till the offering is taken at church to decide what you are going to give. An offering needs to be prepared for. It is a time of worship.

Upon the first day of the week let every one of you lay by him in store, as God hath prospered him . . .
(1 Corinthians 16:2)

REFLECTION POINTS

Sometimes we need to check up on ourselves. Here are a few reality questions. They are not meant to make you feel uncomfortable. We need to know where and what we spend our time doing and where the treasure is going.

1) How much have you given of your time this past week?

How many hours were spent on the job?	_____ hours
How many hours were spent sleeping?	_____ hours
How many hours were spent watching TV?	_____ hours
How many hours were spent at church?	_____ hours
How many were spent working for God?	_____ hours
Time spent praying and listening to God?	_____ hours
Total hours	_____

There were 168 hours in last week. Do you have a lot of time unaccounted for? Did you watch too much T.V.? Not enough prayer time? Were you satisfied with what you gave your time to?

2) How much treasure did you give to church this Sunday? Did you tithe or give an offering? _____ Both?_____

3) Did you use your talents and gifts this past week? You have multiple talents and gifts. God-given gifts like helps, compassion, encouragement, and talents like singing and writing are skills that transform not only yourself but the whole world around you. How much of your time last week did you spend blessing someone else?

4) Take time this week to write an encouraging note. Maybe take someone to lunch. Use your gifts, talents, and treasure to help someone else. It will be time well spent.

CHAPTER TEN

REALIZE SOME OF GOD'S BEST
HAD THE WORST FAILURES

But we have this treasure in earthen vessels,
that the excellency of the power may be of God,
and not of us (2 Corinthians 4:7).

This wonderful treasure of salvation has God entrusted to earthen vessels. If I had been God, I would have given the charge of the gospel to the Angels. They could have declared it as they did the birth of Jesus; loud, bold, and direct. They would have shined in His radiance and glory as they ministered. But God chose to let fragile human beings be in charge of the Words of life, the gospel. I'm sure it has suffered because of our lack of commitment, our many divisions, and the worldliness that is associated by our humanity. We are weak, easily broken, susceptible to burnout, and moral failure. Yet, God chose to use you and me to carry the precious treasure of this gospel. In the Bible, God never attempted to hide the failures of His leaders. When they repented, God would empower them again and they would do great exploits for the Kingdom.

King David
Anointed Worshipper and Leader

David was one of the greatest men of God in the Bible. He was chosen by God and anointed by the prophet Samuel (1 Samuel 16:13). We know of his exploits as a giant-killer when he single-handed destroyed Goliath with a stone and a sling. In 2 Samuel 6:14, the Bible says,

And David danced before the Lord with all his might . . .

Therefore, we know he was a dedicated worshipper of the Lord. Besides this, he was a gifted musician as he played the harp. However, David was also an adulterer and a premeditated murderer.

David was a success, yet he fell quickly when he strayed from his relationship with the Lord. He committed adultery with Bathsheba and then had Uriah her husband set up to be killed in battle. What a change! From dedicated worshipper, giant-killer, and anointed-King, to a fallen lust-driven executioner.

BUT DAVID REALIZED HIS MISTAKES AND REPENTED OF HIS SINS TO THE LORD.

And Nathan said to David, "Thou art the man." Thus saith the Lord God of Israel, "I anointed thee king over Israel, and I delivered thee out of the hand of Saul" (2 Samuel 12:7).

And David said unto Nathan, "I have sinned against the Lord." And Nathan said unto David, "The Lord also hath put away thy sin; thou shalt not die" (2 Samuel 12:13).

Most likely, David recalled that the Spirit of the Lord had departed from King Saul (1Samuel 16:14). David's heart was broken over his sin, and he cried out to God . . .

Cast me not away from thy presence; and take not thy holy spirit from me (Psalm 51:11).

Psalm 51 is a psalm of David, when Nathan the prophet came to him, after he had gone in to Bathsheba. Watch for the true repentance of David as you read this psalm.

Have mercy upon me, O God, according to thy lovingkindness: according unto the multitude of thy tender mercies blot out my transgressions. Wash me throughly from mine iniquity, and cleanse me from my sin. For I acknowledge my transgressions: and my sin is ever before me. Against thee, thee only, have I sinned, and done this evil in thy sight: that thou mightest be justified when thou speakest, and be clear when thou judgest. Behold, I was

*shapen in iniquity; and in sin did my mother
conceive me. Behold, thou desirest truth in the
inward parts: and in the hidden part thou shalt
make me to know wisdom. Purge me with
hyssop, and I shall be clean: wash me, and I
shall be whiter than snow. Make me to hear joy
and gladness; that the bones which thou hast
broken may rejoice. Hide thy face from my sins,
and blot out all mine iniquities. Create in me a
clean heart, O God; and renew a right spirit
within me. Cast me not away from thy
presence; and take not thy holy spirit from me.
Restore unto me the joy of thy salvation; and
uphold me with thy free spirit. Then will I teach
transgressors thy ways; and sinners shall be
converted unto thee. Deliver me from
bloodguiltiness, O God, thou God of my
salvation: and my tongue shall sing aloud of
thy righteousness. O Lord, open thou my lips;
and my mouth shall shew forth thy praise. For
thou desirest not sacrifice; else would I give it:
thou delightest not in burnt offering. The
sacrifices of God are a broken spirit: a broken
and a contrite heart, O God, thou wilt not
despise. Do good in thy good pleasure unto
Zion: build thou the walls of Jerusalem. Then
shalt thou be pleased with the sacrifices of
righteousness, with burnt offering and whole
burnt offering: then shall they offer bullocks
upon thine altar* (vv. 1-19).

Notice all the different ways David repented before the
Lord. He poured out his heart and soul. He begged God to not

cast him away and not to take away his Holy Spirit from him. This should serve as a model prayer for us if we sin against God.

Remember that David was an anointed psalmist, king and a giant-killer yet he backslid on God.

Mighty Samson
Strong and Courageous

Judges 13-16 tell the story of one of the mightiest and strongest men in the Bible. His name was Samson.

From an early age the spirit of the Lord was upon Samson. Samson began his life dedicated to God. The Lord blessed him and he became a judge to Israel. As you study his life, you will discover how he slowly backslid on God. Little by little, he made wrong turns until he was lost and couldn't find the way back. He went after and desired a wife of the heathens and eventually ended up in a harlot's lap revealing the secret of his relationship with God.

Samson could defeat a thousand Philistine with the jawbone of a donkey but couldn't withstand the advances of one woman. The Philistines captured Samson, put out his eyes, and made him grind grain like an animal in the prison house. There Samson found his way back to God and his hair began to grow again.

The Philistines were having a big party to worship their god Dagon and they called for Samson to mock him. As he was in the arena with thousands of Philistines, He asked God for one more chance to be what he was called to be; a warrior. God being the God of mercy and compassion gave that chance

116

to him. He pulled the arena down on him and all the Philistine lords. He had found his way back to God and did more in the end than he had in the beginning.

> . . . So the dead which he slew at his death were more than they which he slew in his life (Judges 16:30).

Remember that Samson could kill a thousand Philistines with a jawbone of a donkey. He was without question the strongest man ever and he backslid on God.

King Solomon
A Man Full of Wisdom and Riches

Solomon was the wisest man in the entire Bible.

> *So king Solomon exceeded all the kings of the earth for riches and for wisdom* (1 Kings 10:23).

> *And God gave Solomon wisdom and understanding exceeding much, and largeness of heart, even as the sand that is on the sea shore* (1 Kings 4:29).

> *But king Solomon loved many strange women, together with the daughter of Pharaoh, women of the Moabites, Ammonites, Edomites, Zidonians, and Hittites* (1 Kings 11:1).

> *For it came to pass, when Solomon was old, that his wives turned away his heart after other*

gods: and his heart was not perfect with the Lord his God, as was the heart of David his father (1 Kings 11:4).

And Solomon slept with his fathers, and was buried in the city of David his father: and Rehoboam his son reigned in his stead (1 Kings 11:43).

The important lesson here is to remember that Solomon in all his riches and wisdom still backslid on God. More money is not the answer but more of God is.

Apostle Peter
A Man With Special Spiritual Insight

The apostle Peter was part of the inner circle of the Lord's chosen disciples. Several times in Scripture we can read of Peter, James, and John being together with the Lord.

Peter had the faith to walk on water (Matthew 14:29); Peter had special spiritual insight (Matthew 16:17); Peter is mentioned first in all four lists of the apostles, yet, the apostle **Peter denied the Lord three times.**

The apostle Peter was probably the most noted failure in Scripture, especially among the disciples. What makes his story important is that he recovered from his failure to serve the Lord in a magnificent way with extraordinary results. Let's look at the scripture.

And the Lord said, "Simon, Simon, behold, Satan hath desired to have you, that he may sift you as wheat: But I have prayed for thee, that thy faith fail not: and when thou art converted, strengthen thy brethren. And he said unto him, Lord, I am ready to go with thee, both into prison, and to death. And he said, I tell thee, Peter, the cock shall not crow this day, before that thou shalt thrice deny that thou knowest me (Luke 22:31-34).

Notice that the Lord knew and forewarned Peter how he would fail. He knew when he would fail and he knew that he would overcome his failure and strengthen others because of it.

The Lord knows our hearts. Nothing can be hidden from Him. We need to be honest with Him and ourselves. Peter was convinced that he would go the distance with the Lord, even unto death. So what do I do when I fail?

If you fail, admit it. When you fail, realize where you went wrong. Don't try to make an excuse. George Washington said, "Ninety-nine percent of failures come from people who have a habit of making excuses."

We can't find help for our mistakes if we are too busy making excuses for them. When you fail, be truly sorry for you failure.

So Peter went out and wept bitterly (Luke 22:62).

As we have said earlier, but it is worth saying again: When you fail, Satan will try to tell you, "What you did wasn't wrong." When you fail, Satan will try to tell you, "It was wrong, but it's no big deal." When you fail, Satan will try to tell you, "It's no use trying again." When you fail, Satan will try to tell you, "God doesn't love you anymore but Satan is a liar!"

There were identifying factors that Peter was backsliding. As long as he was with the Lord, he was bold. He said things like, "I'll never be offended by you" and "I'm ready to go with you to prison or death." He even cut off the high priest's servant's ear when they came to take away the Lord. When Christ was removed and taken captive, Peter was distanced from the Lord. Without Christ close by, he soon resorted to cursing and swearing. Finally, he went back to fishing and took others with him. The Lord, after His resurrection, made a special effort to locate Peter in order to restore him.

> . . . he is risen; he is not here: behold the place where they laid him. But go your way, tell his disciples and Peter that he goeth before you into Galilee: there shall ye see him . . . (Mark 16:6-7).

Remember that Peter was on the inside, had spiritual insight, and walked on water, yet he backslid on the Lord.

It can happen to anyone.
It can happen to any person.
It can even happen to a minister.

A REAL LIFE STORY OF A BACKSLIDER

(The following testimony is in a pastor's own words).

"Completely understand that no one is exempt from falling from grace. Everyone must deal with circumstances and try to keep a grip on his or her salvation. Many think that they are secure from failing but we understand Matthew indicated, "For there shall arise false Christs, and false prophets, and shall shew great signs and wonders; insomuch that, if it were possible, they shall deceive the very elect" (Matthew 24:24).

With that being said, I would like to share that this actually happened to me many years ago while pastoring in Atlanta, Georgia. I was so busy with the activities that I began to slack in my prayer life. This affected my marriage, my finances, and my family. The stress of failure in my walk with God was an embarrassment to me, which in turn caused me to slip in my walk with the Lord. I felt like a complete disappointment to the kingdom of God which led me to almost leave ministry.

After much discouragement, I resigned my church and accepted a job back in my hometown. Several weeks had passed by after leaving my church, and I was very broken in my spirit. I felt very lost and uncertain in anything. It's at this point I realized I had personally backslidden in my walk with the Lord.

Once I recognized the state I was in, I immediately fell on my knees and asked the Lord to forgive my sins of apathy, insecurity, and doubt. We must acknowledge our weaknesses and come to terms that life is not life without the King being king. After repenting of my sins I immediately felt restored and renewed. It was just a few weeks later that we had a call from a very prestigious church in central Florida that wanted us to be their pastor of student ministries. This was a full-time position in one of the largest churches in Florida. I acknowledge that God always has a plan for each of us to identify the state of our walk and recalibrate ourselves to get in line where the Lord desires us to be. I am reminded of an old saying, 'Get underneath the spout where the glory is coming out.'

The Lord has been very gracious to me through the years. I have had the privilege of preaching around the world and seeing many people come to know the Lord. I pray that this simple testimony will encourage your walk and help you to keep from backsliding. If you are in a backslidden state know that God desires you to be back in fellowship with him. Take the steps necessary to reconnect with the Lord and be in the center of His will."

—Mike Carson Jr.

Today Pastor Mike is a full-time pastor and evangelist who holds a license of the rank of bishop in the Church of God. He is a living testimony to the grace and mercy of God. God will restore the fallen. Praise the Lord!

Let's Sum It Up!

We must realize that some of God's greatest followers had some miserable failures. We must recognize that we are capable of outlandish failures ourselves. If we think we are not capable of backsliding, the trap is already being set.

Wherefore let him that thinketh he standeth take heed lest he fall (1 Corinthians 10:12).

We are not stronger or more courageous than Samson neither are we wiser or richer than Solomon. We surely are not more of an anointed giant killer than David was. Our spiritual insight is not any better than the apostle Peter. We surely don't think we are better than any of these great men in the Word of God. We must not think we are beyond failure and backsliding.

We can learn from their mistakes and ours. These examples are given so we can have hope after we have fallen. We cannot use them as excuses or evidence that this is acceptable behavior. It is possible to backslide but also it is feasible to stay true to God. If you have backslid and returned to God, then thanks are due to God for an undeserved second chance. If a backslider doesn't return to God quickly, he will get worse and he will lead a miserable life. The only hope for the sinner, or the backslider, is to turn to God.

For if after they have escaped the pollutions of the world through the knowledge of the Lord and Saviour Jesus Christ, they are again entangled therein, and overcome, the latter end is worse with them than the beginning. For it had been better for them not to have known the way of righteousness, than, after they have known it, to turn from the holy commandment delivered unto them. But it is happened unto them according to the true proverb, The dog is turned to his own vomit again; and the sow that was washed to her wallowing in the mire (2 Peter 2:20-22).

The apostle Paul was concerned about backsliding. He said in 1 Corinthians 9:27 "But I keep under my body, and bring it into subjection: lest that by any means, when I have preached to others, I myself should be a castaway."

The writer of Hebrews was concerned about going back, He said in Hebrews 10:38, "Now the just shall live by faith: but if any man draw back, my soul shall have no pleasure in him."

Jude was concerned about us holding on to our faith. He said in Jude 1:3, "Beloved, when I gave all diligence to write unto you of the common salvation, it was needful for me to write unto you, and exhort you that ye should earnestly contend for the faith which was once delivered unto the saints."

***We* need to be concerned also.**

REFLECTION POINTS

1) Backsliding happens. Have you ever backslid on the Lord? What was a primary factor that attributed to you going backwards in your Christian walk?

2) Do you know anyone who backslid and came back to God? Ask that person to tell you his story.

3) Do you know anyone who was a Christian and backslid and is still away from the Lord? How is that working out for him? Is he happy? Does he seem fulfilled in life?

4) People don't backslide overnight; they grow cold—a degree at a time. Which of the following do you think are the identifying factors to a person losing out with God?

Prayerlessness − Bitterness − Mediocre Church Attendance

Deficient Bible Reading − Little Giving − No Commitment

Gossiping − Evil Thinking − Lack of a Servant's Heart

5) Now go back to number 4 and list 1-9 the issue that you have the MOST problem with. Number 1 being the greatest and Number 9 being the least. Put a number over the identifying factor.

CHAPTER ELEVEN

THE PRODIGAL PRINCIPLE
I will arise and go to my Father.

God gave us an incredible example of a backslider and his return to the Father in His Word. There are many wonderful truths shadowed in this biblical account. Some think this is a parable; however, it is not stated to be a parable. In fact, it says, "a certain man had two sons." Either way, it is a biblical truth that we can rely on. You may find yourself in this story. Let us look at the scriptures.

> *And he said, "A certain man had two sons: And the younger of them said to his father, 'Father, give me the portion of goods that falleth to me.'*

And he divided unto them his living. And not many days after the younger son gathered all together, and took his journey into a far country, and there wasted his substance with riotous living. And when he had spent all, there arose a mighty famine in that land; and he began to be in want. And he went and joined himself to a citizen of that country; and he sent him into his fields to feed swine. And he would fain have filled his belly with the husks that the swine did eat: and no man gave unto him. And when he came to himself, he said, 'How many hired servants of my father's have bread enough and to spare, and I perish with hunger! I will arise and go to my father, and will say unto him, "Father, I have sinned against heaven, and before thee, And am no more worthy to be called thy son: make me as one of thy hired servants."' And he arose, and came to his father. But when he was yet a great way off, his father saw him, and had compassion, and ran, and fell on his neck, and kissed him. And the son said unto him, Father, I have sinned against heaven, and in thy sight, and am no more worthy to be called thy son. But the father said to his servants, "Bring forth the best robe, and put it on him; and put a ring on his hand, and shoes on his feet: And bring hither the fatted calf, and kill it; and let us eat, and be merry: For this my son was dead, and is alive again; he was lost, and is found." And they began to be merry (Luke 15:11-24).

Here are some reflections on this wonderful story.

The Prodigal Son was allowed to leave. This was a step of choice. He was not an outcast. He was not a stranger. He was part of the family. He was with the father. He was in the safety of the home. He didn't cease being the son when he left, even though he was out of the will of the father. He depicts the true backslider. Unlike the pagan or sinner who has never known the good way, he represents the son who left home.

In the beginning we have a choice to serve God or not. God, at salvation, does not take away our power of choice. If anything, the power of choice is increased. Two thieves hung on the cross with Christ. They are to remind us that there are only two choices. One to accept Christ and one to decline; one went to hell. He reminds us that we can never presume that because we are close to the King that we are automatically included in the Kingdom; one to paradise. He assures that even in our last moments on earth, when we acknowledge Him, He will remember us. It is your choice.

When the Prodigal Son left, he was on his own. That was a step of independence. Even though he was still the son, he was now outside the blessings of being at home. When he was home, he had the constant protection and oversight of the father. Now that he is gone, he is left to his own demise. Without the leading hand of his father, he eventually spent all his inheritance. There was a famine and he began to be in want. Nothing seems to go right when you are out of God's will. It is one thing to be a sinner but another to be a backslider and have known the blessings of the Christian life.

He never meant this to happen. He had hoped for success. But once again sin took him farther than he planned to go, kept him longer than he intended to stay and charged him more than he wanted to pay. This is the nature of sin and the life of a backslider.

Romans 6:23 says, "For the wages of sin is death; but the gift of God is eternal life through Jesus Christ our Lord."

Proverbs 11:19 says, "As righteousness tendeth to life: so he that pursueth evil pursueth it to his own death."

The Prodigal Son had to come to himself. This was a step of responsibility. At some point when he was in the pig pen of his demise, the scripture says, "he came to himself." Too often, we want to blame everyone else for our problems. Many times it is our own fault. We made the choices that brought us to the pig pen. We blame the economy, our friends, our enemies, our parents, our spouse, our children, the church, the preacher, and many times even God. Our "self" is usually the last one on the list. The first step toward home is when we have come to our "self" on the list to blame. It is easy to play the "Blame game."

- We blame the banker when we can't get a loan.
  It may be our fault for not paying our bills on time.
- We blame the doctor when we are sick.
  We may be sick because of our abusive lifestyle.
- We blame the policeman for giving us a ticket.
  We got the ticket because we broke the law.
- We blame the preacher for our guilty feelings.
  We are the ones who have sinned.
- We blame the devil for our sin.

The Bible says we are drawn away by our own lust.

Two boys were eating lunch one day and one said, "Bologna again today. This is the third day in a row that I have had bologna. I'm getting tired of bologna!" The other kid said, "Why don't you tell your mom to fix you something else." The first kid replied, "Why tell my mom, I fix my own lunch!" Most of us fix our own lunch also.

The Prodigal Son made a choice to return. This was a step of reasoning. Life is full of choices. Each road we take in life has splits, turns, and detours and each one brings a new choice. The choices that you make will affect your future. The power to choose is a great gift from God. We must be careful to choose wisely.

Be careful who you choose to follow.
> *Envy thou not the oppressor, and choose none of his ways* (Proverbs 3:31).

Be careful of the life you choose to live.
> *I call heaven and earth to record this day against you, that I have set before your life and death, blessing and cursing: therefore choose life, that both thou and thy seed may live* (Deuteronomy. 30:19).

> *That which is altogether just shalt thou follow, that thou mayest live, and inherit the land which the Lord thy God giveth thee* (Deuteronomy 16:20).

Be careful the words you choose to say.

Death and life are in the power of the tongue: and they that love it shall eat the fruit thereof (Proverbs 18:21).

Be careful the God you choose to serve.

And if it seem evil unto you to serve the Lord, choose you this day whom ye will serve; whether the gods which your fathers served that were on the other side of the flood, or the gods of the Amorites, in whose land ye dwell: but as for me and my house, we will serve the Lord (Joshua 24:15).

Once Lincoln was asked how he was going to treat the rebellious southerner when they had finally been defeated and had returned to the Union of the United States. The questioner expected that Lincoln would take a dire vengeance, but he answered, "I will treat them as if they had never been away." (The Gospel of Luke, William Berkley).

The Prodigal Son knew the way home. This was the step of remembrance. There is a well-worn path to the door of the father. Home is the same place where we leave it. The father never sold the farm. Thank God for all the saints who never sold the farm. While some have drifted away, there are those who have maintained the farm. It is waiting on the return of the Prodigal. It is an old path. The landmarks are still readable.

Cause me to hear thy lovingkindness in the morning; for in thee do I trust: cause me to know the way wherein I should walk; for I lift up my soul unto thee (Psalm 143:8).

*And whither I go ye know, and **the way ye know** (John 14:4).*

*For every one that asketh receiveth; **and he that seeketh findeth**; and to him that knocketh it shall be opened* (Luke 11:10).

The father was waiting for his return. This was the step of grace. The father stood at the door with open arms ready to run toward the Prodigal. The father's feet of forgiveness always run faster than the son's steps of repentance. It is not the will of God that any should perish (Matthew 18:14). God has our best interest in mind. He is thinking good thoughts toward us (Jeremiah 29:11). Christ has done His part. He gave His life as a ransom for our soul. Now it is our turn to come to Him. He is waiting

REFLECTION POINTS

Across Clues

1. _____ and death
5. allowed to leave
7. where he went
8. where he ended up
9. the prodigal had one

Down Clues

2. the party animal
3. blessing and_____
4. he came to _____
6. the gift of God

CHAPTER TWELVE

SO, WHAT DO I DO NOW?

Do your first works over!

I f you have been away from God for any length of time and have fallen deep into sin, it probably is a good idea to do some things over again. Sometimes our struggle in our faith is because we did not follow through with our commitment to God.

> *Remember therefore from whence thou art fallen, and repent, and do the first works; or else I will come unto thee quickly, and will remove thy candlestick out of his place, except thou repent* (Revelation 2:5).

This great church of Ephesus that is referred to in Revelation 2 was the same one that the apostle Paul started in Acts 19. It had a tremendous beginning. The believers were baptized in water and baptized in the Holy Ghost. They studied the word daily and prayed. However, they had fallen. The command of the Lord was to repent and remember and DO YOUR FIRST WORKS OVER. This is what you are doing. You are starting over again. What are some of the "first works" that Jesus told them to do again?

Get Baptized in water.

Therefore we are buried with him by baptism into death: that like as Christ was raised up from the dead by the glory of the Father, even so we also should walk in newness of life. For if we have been planted together in the likeness of his death, we shall be also in the likeness of his resurrection (Romans 6:4-5).

Salvation is a wonderful free gift from God. It cannot be bought or earned. It is strictly by grace and through faith that we are saved and not of works lest any man should boast (Ephesians 2:8, 9). Water baptism is my first opportunity to do something in response to this great gift from God. It is my public confession of my salvation. It is a statement of my new life as a new creature in Christ. It is a performance of Christ resurrection through me. It is a testimony that the Church lives on and an act of thanks for God's gift of salvation. God has done for me what I could not do and now this is my first opportunity to do something for Him. I will follow Him in baptism. I am testifying of being born again.

Buried with him in baptism, wherein also ye are risen with him through the faith of the operation of God, who hath raised him from the dead (Colossians 2:12).

There may be many reasons why a person would not want to be baptized. I can think of at least three. One is **fear**. Some people are terrified of water. This is called Aquaphobia. Aquaphobia is among the top 10 phobias in the world according to a study conducted by the National Institute of Mental Health (NIMH) and affects roughly one in every 50 people on the earth. Fear can extend also to the fear of people. Some are so timid, shy, and backward that is will affect their decisions, which affects their life.

The second one is that some think it is **not necessary** to be baptized. Baptism is as necessary as any other act of obedience to the gospel. Is it necessary to love God with all your heart or to love your neighbor as yourself? If you accepted Christ and died before you had the opportunity to show your love for God or your neighbor, I'm sure you would go to heaven. However, given the time and opportunity to demonstrate your love and you refused to love God, the end result would be different. Therefore, when given the chance and challenge of baptism, one should respond and submit to the gospel and with joy be baptized.

The third and most common is **lack of commitment**. It does take time and some planning to be baptized. I have found that most times, those who are not willing to make the necessary commitment to be baptized are not ready for the commitment that it will take to be a Christian. It will take

136

more dedication to carry the cross than to get into the water. However when a person is willing to follow the Lord in baptism, they will have the strength to carry the cross when the time comes.

Seek the Baptism of the Holy Ghost.

The baptism in the Holy Ghost, the Holy Spirit, being endued with power, filled with His Spirit, accepting the promise of the Father, or receiving the gift of the Spirit are just a few references to the Holy Ghost. What is this Holy Ghost? First of all, he is not a what, He is a who.

The Holy Ghost is the third person of the triune Godhead. First John 5:7 says, "For there are three that bear record in heaven, the Father, the Word, and the Holy Ghost: and these three are one."

There are many good books and much study material concerning the Holy Spirit. The Holy Spirit is something a person must experience. The first thing a believer needs to do is spend time praying and tarrying for the indwelling of the Spirit.

And I will pray the Father, and he shall give you another Comforter, that he may abide with you for ever (John 14:16).

The Holy Spirit is a gift from our heavenly Father. Jesus said, "If ye then, being evil, know how to give good gifts unto your children: how much more shall your heavenly Father give the Holy Spirit to them that ask him?" (Luke 11:13).

137

The baptism of the Holy Spirit is essential to be an overcomer. Acts 1:8 says, "But ye shall receive power, after that the Holy Ghost is come upon you: and ye shall be witnesses unto me both in Jerusalem, and in all Judaea, and in Samaria, and unto the uttermost part of the earth."

This Promise of the Holy Spirit was for the disciples (Luke 24:49). The promise was for the people at Pentecost (Acts 2:37-38) and more importantly this promise is for you. The Scripture ensures us that the promise is for all Christians.

> *For the promise is unto you, and to your children, and to all that are afar off, even as many as the Lord our God shall call* (Acts 2:39).

You are a candidate for the baptism. If you have never been baptized, then seek the baptism in the Holy Spirit. If it has been a while since the Holy Spirit has been evident in your life then seek to do the first works again. Let it be a fresh encounter with the presence of God. Seek the Lord with all your heart. Don't seek the baptism only, but rather, seek the baptizer.

In one of his meetings, D.L. Moody was explaining to his audience the truth that we cannot bring about spiritual changes in our lives by our own strength. He demonstrated the principle like this: "Tell me," he said to his audience, "how can I get the air out of the tumbler I have in my hand?" One man said, "Suck it out with a pump." But Moody replied, "That would create a vacuum and shatter it." Finally after many suggestions, he picked up a pitcher and quietly filled the

138

glass with water. "There," he said, "all the air is now removed." He then explained that victory for the child of God does not come by working hard to eliminate sinful habits, but rather by allowing Christ to take full possession.

Get back to the Basics.

Brother Kenny, a preacher friend of mine said, "If you want to be a good Christian and keep the devil out of your life, you need to do five things; Pray, read your Bible, go to church, pay your tithes, and witness." That seems pretty simple but it holds a lot of truth. It is not a hard thing to serve the Lord. Our God will lead you, the Holy Spirit will live in you, the Word will guide you, the Lord will walk beside you, and the church will help you. You can make it. Matter of fact, you are destined to be the head and not the tail. You are more than conqueror because ". . . greater is He that is in you than he that is in the world" (1 John 4:4),

Hopefully, this time we have shared together will put you back on track. These disciplines are very basic and simple. It does not take a rocket scientist to understand these precepts and principles, but it will take determination to implement them.

REFLECTION POINTS

This chapter was about "What do I do now?" Sometimes we need to evaluate what we have done in order to recognize what needs to be next. Complete the Spiritual Checklist below and it should help you chart a course for your Spiritual walk with the Lord.

A Personal Spiritual Checklist

1) Been Born Again .... Yes____No____

2) Been Baptized in Water .... Yes____No____

3) Been Baptized in the Holy Spirit .... Yes____No____

4) Been Reading My Bible .... Yes____No____

5) Attending a Good Church .... Yes____No____

6) Have a Daily Devotion .... Yes____No____

7) Have a Daily Prayer time .... Yes____No____

8) Have a Mentor .... Yes____No____

9) Have a Covenant Partner .... Yes____No____

10) Pay my Tithes .... Yes____No____

11) Been a witness to someone .... Yes____No____

CHAPTER THIRTEEN

TWO LAST WORDS

Be a Giver

We have already covered the fact that we were saved to be givers in chapter nine. However, this cannot be stressed enough. This world has trained us to be a taker. We are conditioned to believe that we deserve success. Slogans like, "You deserve a break today" and "Have it your way" are engrained into the fiber of our being. When is the last time that you heard a commercial that said, "Don't think of yourself" or "Let someone else have it their way"? This is what the gospel is about. Jesus talked of taking up our cross, being servants, and loving our neighbor like we love ourselves. Even though it is not in the Bible, there is a

"Golden Rule" that says, "Do unto others as you would have them do unto you."

> *Every man according as he purposeth in his heart, so let him give; not grudgingly, or of necessity: for God loveth a **cheerful** giver* (2 Corinthians 9:7).

> *I have shewed you all things, how that so labouring ye ought to support the weak, and to remember the words of the Lord Jesus, how he said, "It is more **blessed** to give than to receive"* (Acts 20:35).

> *Not because I desire a gift: but I desire **fruit** that may abound to your account* (Philippians 4:17).

When we focus on others, we will notice the manifestation of purpose and prosperity becoming evident in our lives. Words like cheerful, blessed and fruitful become who we are. This is because our giving to God and others results in God and others giving to us. What we give away always comes back in greater quantity.

Sometimes we assume giving only benefits the one who is receiving the gift; however, the real recipient of the good is the giver. It becomes fruit that is put in our eternal account. God said "whatsoever a man sows, that shall he reap." If you plant bad things in life, you will receive bad things. If you sow good, you will reap a harvest of good. Become a giver. It will abound to your account, and you can make many withdrawals because you walk with God. Luke 6:38 says,

Give, and it shall be given unto you; good measure, pressed down, and shaken together, and running over, shall men give into your bosom. For with the same measure that ye mete withal it shall be measured to you again.

Someone once said, "What you make happen for others, God will make happen for you." God said this a long time ago in His Word. Isaiah 58:10-12 says,

And if thou draw out thy soul to the hungry, and satisfy the afflicted soul; then shall thy light rise in obscurity, and thy darkness be as the noonday. And the Lord shall guide thee continually, and satisfy thy soul in drought, and make fat thy bones: and thou shalt be like a watered garden, and like a spring of water, whose waters fail not. And they that shall be of thee shall build the old waste places: thou shalt raise up the foundations of many generations; and thou shalt be called, The repairer of the breach, The restorer of paths to dwell in.

With good will doing service, as to the Lord, and not to men: Knowing that whatsoever good thing any man doeth, the same shall he receive of the Lord, whether he be bond or free (Ephesians 6:7-8).

Open up your hands and be a giver. We come out of our mother's womb with a clinched fist. Even as little babies we grab hold of our mom's finger and hold on to it tight. When

144

we were toddlers we were grabbing rattlers and other toys but when another infant drew near, we would say, "No, that's mine." Everything throughout our lives came with handles because we are natural clutchers. Only when we die do we relax our grip and open our hands. Let's not wait till death, do it now, become a giver.

BE A FORGIVER.

And when ye stand praying, forgive, if ye have ought against any: that your Father also which is in heaven may forgive you your trespasses (Mark 11:25).

Forgive Others.
(The Process of Mercy)

When you decide to pray, let forgiveness be first on the list. You won't be able to hold God's hand and a grudge at the same time.

If you want to endure to the end of your journey, you will need to unpack all your grudges. There is no heavier load that you will carry than hurt feelings. It is like drag racing with the parking brake on or running a marathon with a ball and chain. Unforgiveness is like a deadly cancer that will eat you up on the inside and eventually destroy you if it is not eradicated. Unforgiveness traps you in the past and robs you of a joyful future.

The best gift to give yourself today is to forgive everyone you know including yourself. Most people try to get even with their enemies but it is better to get ahead of them. You do that by forgiving them first. Forgive them before they forgive you. Be a winner. Forgive first.

> *The only people you should try to get even with are those who have helped you* (anonymous).

The apostle Peter questioned the Lord concerning how many times we are to forgive our brother. Peter suggested seven times but the Lord said, "Seven times seventy" was more like it. There were to be **NO LIMITS** on forgiveness.

As a Christian we are to be imitators of God. We will never be more like God than when we are giving and forgiving. John 3:16 says, "For God so loved the world, that he gave his only begotten Son, that whosoever believeth in him should not perish, but have everlasting life." In this well-known verse we see both the giver and the forgiver. God so loved that He gave His son and if you believe, He forgives.

> Our God overflows with mercy. Psalm 103:17 says, *"But the **mercy of the Lord is from everlasting to everlasting** upon them that fear him, and his righteousness unto children's children."*

> *O give thanks unto the Lord; for he is good: **for his mercy endureth for ever*** (Psalm 118:29).

> *The earth, O Lord, is **full of thy mercy**: teach me thy statutes* (Psalm 119:64).

God has forgiven us and He will help us to forgive others. We have obtained mercy; we need to be merciful or full of mercy ourselves. Luke 6:36 says, "Be ye therefore merciful, as your Father also is merciful."

God has forgiven us a great debt and expects us to forgive others. The Bible says in Mark 11:25, "And when ye stand praying, forgive, if ye have ought against any: that your Father also which is in heaven may forgive you your trespasses." When we have unforgiveness in our heart, it stops the flow of forgiveness into our life. This can be one of the hardest things you will ever do but it has to be done. Set down today and write that letter, make the phone call or go in person and cancel someone's debt that they owe you. I know they owe you the apology. Forgive them anyway. The person that will be set free is you. You will feel so much better. God will help you. Do it today.

Forgive Yourself.
(The Acceptance of Grace)

Make sure you don't forget to forgive yourself. Nobody knows the depth of my sin better than me. I alone know how sinful I can be. I must accept the grace and mercy of God when He forgives. I am not the faithful one, He is. The Scripture says in 1 John 1:9, "If we confess our sins, he is faithful and just to forgive us our sins, and to cleanse us from all unrighteousness." Let me say it again, I confess, and God is **faithful** to forgive. Don't allow yourself or others to hold you hostage for your past sins. When you confess, God will forgive and you must let them go. God has put them behind His back and so should you.

As far as the east is from the west, so far hath he removed our transgressions from us (Psalm 103:12).

Behold, for peace I had great bitterness: but thou hast in love to my soul delivered it from the pit of corruption: for thou hast cast all my sins behind thy back (Isaiah 38:17).

When it comes to forgiving oneself, it is easy to substitute penance for repentance. We blame ourselves for our past mistakes and it becomes a form of self-punishment and should make us feel better but it doesn't. Prolonged guilty feelings will enslave and condemn you. Christ died to bring forgiveness to you. It is a spiritual gift that only freedom comes when you forgive yourself.

There is therefore now no condemnation to them which are in Christ Jesus, who walk not after the flesh, but after the Spirit. For the law of the Spirit of life in Christ Jesus hath made me free from the law of sin and death (Romans 8:1-2).

Without a doubt the hardest person to forgive lives the closest to you, knows you better than anyone else, and you have to look at him or her every day. Accept the grace of God and move on. With one feeble step in front of the other, move on. It may be all uphill and you may move slowly but you must move on. You may have to move something aside so you can move on. Someday we will move up but for now we have to move on. You may have to **Start Over, Again** in order to move on. Let's move on!

Don't Quit

When things go wrong as they sometimes will
When the road you're trudging seems all up hill,
When funds are low and the debts are high,
And you want to smile, but you have to sigh.
When care is pressing you down a bit,
Rest, if you must, but don't you quit.
Life is queer with its twists and turns,
As everyone of us sometimes learns.
And many a failure turns about,
When he might have won had he stuck it out.

Don't give up though the pace seems slow,
You may succeed with another blow.
Success is failure turned inside out,
The silver tint of the clouds of doubt.
And you never can tell how close you are,
It may be near when it seems so far.
So stick to the fight when you're hardest hit,
It's when things seem worst that you must not QUIT.

(Author unknown)

About the Author

Rick Cottrell, pastor, teacher, evangelist, founder of Eagles Ridge Ministries and wannabe writer has been "born again" for over 39 years. He is currently serving as the pastor of the Linden Church of God in Linden, Tennessee. He has been there for the past 25 years. He regularly preaches revivals and participates in camp meetings and conferences.

He holds the ministry rank of bishop in the Church of God denomination, Cleveland, Tennessee. Within his denomination he has had the opportunity to serve on several boards and committees including the State Evangelism Board, State Youth Board, State Council and as a Pastoral Covenant Facilitator.

He considers being married to his wonderful wife Pam for the past 35 years to be the highlight of his life. Together, they have two wonderful daughters, Brittany and Kelly. They are gifts from God.

Contact information:
Eagles Ridge Ministries
Pastor Rick Cottrell
P.O. Box 317
Linden, TN 37096
www.eaglesridgeministries.org
email-brorickc@gmail.com